THE OFFICIAL  GUIDE

GRAND
PRIX 2009»

This edition published in 2009 by
Carlton Books Limited
20 Mortimer Street
London W1T 3JW

10 9 8 7 6 5 4 3 2 1

itv SPORT ▮

A CIP catalogue record for this book is available from
the British Library.

The publisher has taken reasonable steps to check
the accuracy of the facts contained herein at the
time of going to press, but can take no responsibility
for any errors.

ISBN: 978-184732-262-3

Designer: Luke Griffin
Picture Research: Paul Langan
Production: Lucca Bazzoli
Project Art Editor: Paul Chattaway

Printed and bound in the United Kingdom
by Butler Tanner & Dennis Ltd, Frome

Formula One's ever-increasing global expansion adds another new flag to its roster this year with Abu Dhabi hosting a grand prix for the first time to bring the championship to a close.

THE OFFICIAL itv SPORT GUIDE

GRAND PRIX 2009》》

BRUCE JONES

CARLTON
BOOKS

CONTENTS

LEFT: Pit stops never fail to provide a blur of colour and excitement. This is Nelson Piquet Jr powering away from one in 2008.
OVERLEAF: Ferraris and Fernando Alonso's Renault were to the fore in the 2008 Spanish GP. Will it be the same this time around?

ANALYSIS OF THE 2009 SEASON

Formula One was prepared for one of its occasional new rolls of the dice, with a set of technical regulations being imposed to spice up the racing. Then the global economic crisis hit and Honda Racing quit. Urgent meetings were held and a raft of cost-saving rule changes have been made that might shake up the order further.

So, what's new? The first thing that you will notice is that the cars look different in reaction to suggestions by the Overtaking Working Group. Gone are the winglets that festooned the cars and their bargeboards too, as well as the chimneys that made the sidepods lumpy. Underneath the rear, the 2009 diffuser is longer, higher and moved further back. The rear wing is a fraction of the size to which we've become accustomed, being 25cm narrower and sitting much higher than before, with its top edge level with the top of the engine cover. The front wing sits lower than before, but is wider, with 40cm being added to its width. Best of all, the front wing's centre section is driver-adjustable, and they will be able to raise or lower the plane twice per lap to improve their chances of getting close enough to the car in front to overtake. The aim of these changes is to reduce downforce and thus make it easier for drivers to race closer to other cars, thus boosting the number of passing opportunities.

Almost as exciting for older F1 fans is the return of slick tyres. These big, made-for-racing slabs of rubber just look right and,

hopefully, will encourage drivers to throw their cars more vigorously into corners to try and pull off an overtaking manoeuvre.

Hidden within the bodywork is the much talked-about KERS (Kinetic Energy Recovery System). This is effectively an energy storage system that harnesses energy generated by braking. This energy can then be released to boost acceleration, offering as much as 80bhp out of corners

Cost-cutting became essential as the global economy dived, and the result of meetings last December was a host of changes to ensure that no teams followed Honda's rush for the door. The FIA had already proposed a standard engine and spec gearbox for 2010. The teams didn't like this and have instead agreed to augment the previous agreement of making engines last for three grand prix meetings by cutting peak revs to 18,000rpm with no retuning, a decision that's expected to halve the engine budgets for the independent teams. The other changes adopted to achieve a 30% cut to overall budgets were to reduce aerodynamic development by outlawing the use of wind tunnels either larger than 60% in scale or capable of operating at faster than 50m/s. But perhaps the biggest cost-saving will be the banning of in-season testing. The number of staff taken to races will also be cut through the sharing of information about tyres and fuel.

The calendar has been chopped around, losing the Canadian and French GPs, but gaining Abu Dhabi for the season's finale.

Another announcement from the FIA is that all stewards' decisions will come with a written explanation of how they were reached, which really ought to go some way towards making the stewards accountable after some of the seemingly odd and inconsistent decisions they made last year.

One has to presume that Ferrari and McLaren will remain as the standard setters. With unchanged driver line-ups, status quo should be maintained, but McLaren will be hoping that Heiki Kovalainen will move up a gear so that they can gun for the constructors' championship. Equally, Ferrari will hope that 2007 champion Kimi Raikkonen is revitalised and finds the new-style cars more to his liking.

BMW Sauber has one of Formula One's jewels in Robert Kubica: quick, mistake-free and ruthless, but the team will have to work out how to match the development pace of the top two teams.

Renault came on strong with their former champion Fernando Alonso late last year and is sure to be competitive again. There were signs that Toyota was coming good last year and it has two rapid drivers in Jarno Trulli and the fast-improving Timo Glock. Again, it's wonderfully hard to predict where teams will place, as the midfield has become increasingly congested, so perhaps billionaire Vijay Mallya will have helped Force India take its battle to Red Bull, Toro Rosso and Williams by signing up to run Mercedes power trains.

McLAREN

It seems inconceivable that McLaren has not won a constructors' title since 1998, so you can be sure that this is its principal aim for 2009. The drivers' title last year for Lewis Hamilton was great, but this would mean even more to the team from Woking.

If you thought Lewis Hamilton was fast last year, watch out in 2009.

Expect more of the same, only better from McLaren in 2009, as the pressure is off to an extent now that the team, or at least one of its drivers, has a world title again. For a team of McLaren's quality, not winning titles was eating into them. Now, it can go forward, and there is no reason why it can't enter another lengthy period of excellence, as it did in the late 1980s and early 1990s, as everything is in place and there's no spying scandal to distract them.

There's a strong technical team led by Paddy Lowe and head of design & development, Neal Oatley. Mercedes-Benz is as willing a partner as ever and its in-house simulator helps its drivers no end in preparation for the races, its worth shown through the course of last season as the team powered forward through the middle of the season, learning how not to thrash its tyres too much.

World Champion Lewis Hamilton will also be raring to go again, and will surely not drop back after winning the world title, as Kimi Raikkonen did in 2007 with Ferrari. He should instead be liberated by his title success and start piling grand prix wins on at an ever greater rate, and performances like his dominant, controlling victory in the Chinese GP may become the norm.

That leaves the question

TEAM VIPS

RON DENNIS
Few people in the pit lane live, eat and breathe motor racing as Ron does. His famous dedication has helped him climb from working as a mechanic for Cooper in the 1960s to heading the McLaren Group from its grandiose Technology Centre. Team management was where he wanted to be and a good run in Formula Two led to his Project Four team taking over McLaren in 1980 and he propelled the team to the front, winning titles galore, with the group also turning out supercars for the road.

MARTIN WHITMARSH
Chief operating officer of the McLaren group and chief executive officer of its Formula One team, Martin's first venture into high-performance activities was in the aerospace industry. Joining McLaren from BAE Systems in 1989, his first role was as head of operations, but he was promoted to managing director and each new season brings roles of increased importance as he is groomed to eventually take over the whole show from Ron Dennis.

of whether Heikki Kovalainen can get up to speed in the other car, not just to take race wins too, but to score larger helpings of championship points regularly enough to help McLaren make a fulsome charge at the constructors' title. The signs were positive at the start of last season but he did drop away rather as spring turned to summer, no longer able to put one over Hamilton in qualifying, despite his maiden win at the Hungaroring. Perhaps he didn't go backwards, it's just that Hamilton roared ahead. Whatever, this enormously popular and upbeat individual will have spent the winter on the team's simulator at Woking doing everything that he can to boost his understanding of the new-style car, learn how to maximize his two wing-angle changes per lap and every other factor he can think of. After all, no driver will have a hope of beating Hamilton unless they optimize every single element of their driving.

Not all is static, though, as team supremo Ron Dennis continues to be rumoured to be stepping back from the frontline. Already he has passed on more and more of the operational duties to chief executive officer Martin Whitmarsh and apparently more responsibilities are coming Martin's way, as Ron wants to increase his focus on broadening McLaren's base on the road car market, overseeing its P11 sports car and take on Ferrari in that market as well as on the track.

If there remains one weak point with McLaren, it's that they still produce odd calls. Think Germany 2008, with Hamilton being asked not to pit when the safety car was circulating and the extra pressure it left him under.

Two personnel moves were certain when this book closed for press, with longtime team servant Head of Race Operations, Steve Hallam, leaving for pastures new, moving across the Atlantic to work in the equally competitive but very different world of NASCAR.

The other move was Simon Roberts heading to Force India as Chief Operational Officer as part of the team's deal to use McLaren drivetrains.

Ron Dennis is handing ever more responsibility to Martin Whitmarsh.

FOR THE RECORD

Country of origin:	England
Team base:	Woking, England
Telephone:	(44) 01483 728211
Website:	www.mclaren.com
Active in Formula One:	From 1966
Grands Prix contested:	649
Wins:	162
Pole positions:	141
Fastest laps:	137

2008 DRIVERS & RESULTS

Driver	Nationality	Races	Wins	Pts	Pos
Lewis Hamilton	British	18	5	98	1st
Heikki Kovalainen	Finnish	18	1	53	7th

THE TEAM

Team principal:	Ron Dennis
Chief operating officer:	Martin Whitmarsh
Engineering director:	Paddy Lowe
Design & development director:	Neal Oatley
Head of aerodynamics:	Simon Lacey
Chief engineer:	Tim Goss
Head of race operations:	TBC
Team manager:	Dave Ryan
Test drivers:	TBC
Chassis:	MP4-24
Engine:	Mercedes V8
Tyres:	Bridgestone

LEWIS HAMILTON

Lewis Hamilton, World Champion. That's what it can say on his business card, although it couldn't have been any closer last year. This time around, Lewis will want to make shorter work of it and is sure to be more relaxed in going for his second

It took an age after that Brazilian GP shoot-out for Lewis to recover the power of speech, for seldom has the world witnessed a driver who was so numbed by the enormity of what he had just achieved. It's fair to say, though, that no World Champion before him had ever had to go through such a roller-coaster of a race to achieve their goal and to have lost the battle, only to get it back right at the kill.

Those inside the sport were full of praise for the youngest champion. Those outside saw Lewis for another element of who he is: F1's first black World Champion.

Thinking back over Lewis's triumphal season, it had similar ingredients to his rookie year with McLaren, save for the fact that he wasn't fighting his teammate as he had to do with Fernando Alonso. Heikki Kovalainen was far more supportive and, increasingly, not able to match his pace.

There were mistakes that could have cost him dear. People will remember his

Lewis has no intention of stopping at one world title and hopes to hit new heights.

over-anxious driving at the start of the Japanese GP, putting himself in danger to salvage a place he didn't need to save. However, the one that could have haunted him forever was his pit lane crunch in Canada that cost him 15 to 20 points.

Lewis has the speed, he now has confidence and, this year, it can be allied to a more relaxed demeanour, which can only lead to even greater things.

TRACK NOTES

Nationality:	BRITISH
Born:	7 JANUARY 1985, STEVENAGE, ENGLAND
Website:	www.lewishamilton.com
Teams:	McLAREN 2007-2009

CAREER RECORD

First Grand Prix:	2007 AUSTRALIAN GP
Grand Prix starts:	35
Wins:	9
	2007 Canadian GP, United States GP, Hungarian GP, Japanese GP, 2008 Australian GP, Monaco GP, British GP, German GP, Chinese GP
Pole positions:	13
Fastest laps:	3
Points:	207
Honours:	2008 FORMULA ONE WORLD CHAMPION, 2006 GP2 CHAMPION, 2005 EUROPEAN FORMULA THREE CHAMPION, 2003 BRITISH FORMULA RENAULT CHAMPION, 2000 WORLD KART CUP CHAMPION & EUROPEAN FORMULA A KARTING CHAMPION, 1999 ITALIAN INTERCONTINENTAL A KARTING CHAMPION, 1996 McLAREN MERCEDES CHAMPION OF THE FUTURE, 1995 BRITISH CADET KARTING CHAMPION

SINGLED OUT FOR STARDOM

Lewis was such a hit when he started kart racing at eight that it wasn't long before everyone was paying attention. A chance meeting at an awards dinner in 1996 was key to what followed, when he spoke to McLaren boss Ron Dennis and the deal was completed in 1998, with McLaren and Mercedes financing his progress from there. He won everything in karting, then did the same in the junior formulae, with titles in Formula Renault, European Formula Three and GP2. Formula One was next and he was ready just as McLaren had a vacancy for 2007. Joining at the same time as Fernando Alonso gave Lewis imagined parity, but it was the way that he took it to the double World Champion that amazed. He pushed and improved, with only a mad moment from the team in China preventing him from being the first rookie champion.

HEIKKI KOVALAINEN

He took half of his maiden season with Renault to find his feet and was expected to blossom with McLaren last year but, flashes of speed apart, he has so far found wanting at the highest level, although his popularity within the team has kept him in.

McLaren is a team that almost bends over backwards in its mission to run its drivers as equals. Last year, that was hard to do as Lewis Hamilton is so much part of the team. They were prepared to give it a go, though, as Heikki is a very affable, buoyant individual, a genial spirit after the often malevolent Fernando Alonso who so upset the team's equilibrium in 2007.

Yet, despite a couple of fastest laps in the first three grands prix, it was clear that Hamilton had a performance advantage. The team supported Heikki, urged him, cajoled him. They wanted him to deliver, indeed they needed him to deliver.

Then came Heikki's monster smash in the Spanish GP. A wheel rim is thought to have broken and punctured his tyre at 145mph. He was wedged under a tyrewall, and things looked bad. Yet, Heikki bounced back at the Turkish GP and the team reckoned he would have won but for an extra stop to replace a puncture.

Certainly, he was adjudged to be a qualifying specialist in the first half of the

Heikki says he will match Hamilton and expects to be offered the same opportunities.

season, more than giving Hamilton a run for his money, but Hamilton just kept on improving. In the races themselves, the gap became even larger as Heikki had often taken too much out of his tyres in

qualifying and was left to pay the price in the race's opening stint.

Just when Heikki's retention of his drive was being discussed, McLaren announced that he would be staying on and he promptly won the Hungarian GP. Sure, he was helped by Massa retiring near the end and Hamilton having a puncture, but it was timely nonetheless.

Heikki may yet come good in 2009, but beating Hamilton is not going to be easy.

TRACK NOTES

Nationality:	FINNISH
Born: 19 OCTOBER 1981, SUOMUSSALMI, FINLAND	
Website:	www.heikkikovalainen.net
Teams:	RENAULT 2007
	McLAREN 2008-2009

CAREER RECORD	
First Grand Prix:	2007 AUSTRALIAN GP
Grand Prix starts:	35
Wins:	1
	2008 Hungarian GP
Pole positions:	1
Fastest laps:	2
Points:	83
Honours:	2005 GP2 RUNNER-UP, 2004
	FORMULA NISSAN WORLD SERIES CHAMPION,
	2004 CHAMPION OF CHAMPIONS AT RACE OF
	CHAMPIONS, 2000 NORDIC KARTING CHAMPION

FROM NOWHERE TO HERE

Some think that Finland is a backwater, except if you want to go rallying. Keke Rosberg had a nomadic childhood, but Mika Hakkinen, JJ Lehto and Mika Salo were brought up in or near the capital, Helsinki. In comparison, Heikki hails from where there are only trees and lakes. That he got to Formula One from there is remarkable. However, he won the Nordic karting title in 2000, then headed to Britain and made an immediate impact in Formula Renault. He was a star again in Formula Three, ranking third and finishing second at Macau. He tried World Series by Nissan in 2003, ranked second then became champion in 2004. What made his name was when he beat the best of racing and rallying in the multi-discipline Race of Champions in Paris. Runner-up in GP2 in 2005, Heikki was Renault test driver in 2006 before landing a race seat for 2007.

FERRARI

Ferrari was stung last year and is sure to come back stronger still against McLaren in 2009. There were mistakes last year but, with two top drivers, team boss Stefano Domenicali must show that it's not just Jean Todt who can guide the team to glory.

Felipe Massa has new status in the team after his 2008 title bid.

Life without Jean Todt at the helm has turned Ferrari into a very different team. From the outset of his command, Stefano Domenicali has worked on thawing the frosty relationship with McLaren in particular. Indeed, the team's relationship with the press has improved, So, in short, Ferrari is approachable and human once more. And, good grief, it's even working with the other teams, with President Luca di Montezemolo re-engaging to head FOTA (the Formula One Teams' Association).

ITV commentator James Allen suggested during last year's Chinese GP that perhaps Ferrari had been "driver-limited" in 2008, saying that some in the paddock felt that neither Felipe Massa nor Kimi Raikkonen had got the best out of a very good car. The fact that they claimed the constructors' title and came within a blink of the drivers' crown means that their car was mighty. Indeed, the F2008 was an aerodynamic masterpiece, a car that seemingly could achieve downforce without creating a great deal of drag. It was fast, it was efficient, and the Ferrari V8 engine was a gem. Like all cars, it had a weak point, and that was getting heat into its tyres if conditions were less than steaming hot.

TEAM VIPS

STEFANO DOMENICALI
The man holding the reins at Ferrari since Jean Todt moved on is a racing man through and through. Born in Imola, he watched races as a child before joining his favourite team, Ferrari, straight from university. That was in 1991 and he worked on the management side, also running Ferrari's Mugello circuit, until he was made team manager in 1998, being promoted to sporting director in 2003 and then team principal at the end of 2007.

ALDO COSTA
The man in charge of all things technical at Ferrari is a mechanical engineering graduate who honed his skills with Abarth before joining Minardi in 1988, where he advanced from being a stress engineer to become chief designer. In 1996, Aldo joined Ferrari to run its road car design office. Back in racing in 2005, he was made its Formula One chief designer and then technical director for 2007 after Ross Brawn's departure on a sabbatical.

So, how good will the F2009 be? This is a good question, as all the teams are faced with a vastly different set of aerodynamic regulations with which to work. Expect Ferrari to produce another car that extracts the maximum from the outline rules. If there is an Achilles' heel, rumour has it that this will be its use of KERS as they were said to be lagging behind other teams in this interesting new power storage and release scheme last autumn,

The drivers are known factor, and excellent they are too. What will be interesting to see in the months ahead is how the status quo within the team has to be adjusted if Raikkonen gets back to his best and whether Ferrari can still take the battle to Lewis Hamilton and McLaren if both of its drivers are firing on all cylinders.

There were glitches last year, which was unusual for Ferrari, such as when it really dropped the ball with its tyre choice at the British GP. There was also the pair of engine failures, traced to a rogue batch of conrods. And then, of course, there were pit stop protocol problems at the European and Singapore GPs. The dropping of its traffic lights system followed and you can be sure that a winter of research and development has gone into a superior, fail-safe system.

One other sign of the revolution that Domenicali is forging at Ferrari is that it is finally planning to start a programme to develop future talent, with an F1 test organised for the top three drivers in the Italian Formula Three championship. Well, it certainly worked for McLaren and its hand-picked junior: Hamilton.

FOR THE RECORD

Country of origin:	Italy
Team base:	Maranello, Italy
Telephone:	(39) 0536 949111
Website:	www.ferrariworld.com
Active in Formula One:	From 1950
Grands Prix contested:	776
Wins:	209
Pole positions:	203
Fastest laps:	216

2008 DRIVERS & RESULTS

Driver	Nationality	Races	Wins	Pts	Pos
Felipe Massa	Brazilian	18	6	97	2nd
Kimi Raikkonen	Finnish	18	2	75	3rd

THE TEAM

President:	Luca di Montezemolo
Team principal:	Stefano Domenicali
Technical director:	Aldo Costa
Team manager:	Luca Baldisserri
Engine director:	Gilles Simon
Sporting manager:	Massimo Rivola
Chief designer:	Nicolas Tombazis
Chief aerodynamicist:	John Iley
Race & engine manager:	Mattia Binotto
Test drivers:	Luca Badoer & Marc Gene
Chassis:	Ferrari F2009
Engine:	Ferrari V8
Tyres:	Bridgestone

Stefano Domenicali might need to keep urging Raikkonen on in 2009.

FELIPE MASSA

The images of Felipe's family celebrating in the Ferrari garage at last year's Brazilian GP and then the sudden dawning that the world title had slipped away from him were painful to watch. However, the plucky Brazilian is sure to come back stronger still.

The speed has always been there. Ever since Felipe arrived in Formula One in 2002 with Sauber as something of an unknown. He was a rough diamond and needed polishing. It took time, but the signs in 2006 when he sometimes would outpace Michael Schumacher were there for all to see. Yet it was impossible imagining Felipe doing what he did last year, not only keeping team-mate Kimi Raikkonen in the shade but coming within an ace of landing the world title ahead of Lewis Hamilton.

Still, the facts present themselves and to the accolades earned can be added that of dignity in defeat.

So, going into 2009, Felipe is chock full of confidence and this is something that he has always required to give of his best. Think of grands prix such as those at Valencia and Singapore, when all was right in Felipe's world, and he had the legs on everyone, driving flawlessly. What he must work on to have a chance of a second title shot is how to transform the days when not all is perfect and collect points on

Felipe was transformed from promising to world title-winning material last year.

those occasions rather than, say, spin five times like in last year's wet-dry-wet British GP. Once that matter is addressed, he will become a permanent thorn in Hamilton's side over the years ahead.

If, though, Raikkonen loves the new car and can make it work, it will be interesting to see how Felipe copes with a challenge from within, for he certainly enjoyed the transformation into the focus of Ferrari's attention in the second half of 2008 and would no doubt find internal demotion hard to deal with.

TRACK NOTES

Nationality:	BRAZILIAN
Born:	25 APRIL 1981, SAO PAULO, BRAZIL
Website:	www.felipemassa.com
Teams:	SAUBER 2002 &
	2004-05, FERRARI 2006-09

CAREER RECORD

First Grand Prix:	2002 AUSTRALIAN GP
Grand Prix starts:	106
Grand Prix wins:	11
2006 Turkish GP, Brazilian GP, 2007 Bahrain GP, Spanish GP, Turkish GP, 2008 Bahrain GP, Turkish GP, French GP, Euro GP, Belgian GP, Brazilian GP	
Poles:	15
Fastest laps:	11
Points:	298
Honours:	2008 FORMULA ONE RUNNER-UP, 2001 EUROPEAN FORMULA 3000 CHAMPION, 2000 EUROPEAN & ITALIAN FORMULA RENAULT CHAMPION, 1999 BRAZILIAN FORMULA FORMULA CHEVROLET CHAMPION

THE BOY FROM BRAZIL

It's safe to say that when Sauber signed Felipe for 2002 some of the media didn't know who he was. He hadn't done Formula Three you see. Had they paid more attention, they might have noticed that this baby-faced Brazilian had been Formula Chevrolet champion in 1999 before blitzing European Formula Renault in 2000. He hadn't the money for Formula Three and so did B-category Euro Formula 3000 in 2001 and won at a canter, catching the attention of Peter Sauber who gave him a test and was impressed. He was very fast but very inconsistent compared to team-mate Nick Heidfeld. This is why he was sidelined in 2003, but his manager Nicolas Todt guided him into a test driver role at Ferrari and he learned well so that he was welcomed back to Sauber before joining Ferrari in 2006, occasionally running Michael Schumacher close.

KIMI RAIKKONEN

It was as though Kimi was still in shock last year that he'd come from behind to clinch the 2007 world title, as the Finn won twice in the first four races then never again. He seemed disinterested and this year is key to whether he races on or not.

Examine this statistic if you will. Last year was made up of 18 grands prix and Kimi Raikkonen set the race's fastest lap in 10 of these. You'd expect then that he would have bagged win after win and run away with the drivers' title. But he didn't, he won just two, the Malaysian and Spanish GPs, and was out of the reckoning with two races still to run. More surprising still was that he was outqualified and then outraced by his less fancied team-mate Felipe Massa. So, was he still the Flying Finn, billed as the world's fastest driver, or not?

To many in the pit lane and the media, he was cruising. Indeed, for much of the year there was talk of Kimi quitting at season's end. It stalled the driver market as Fernando Alonso and others eyed the potentially vacant seat at Ferrari.

However, although Kimi has long said that he doesn't plan to stay racing forever, he may yet get the fire in his belly back if he find's this year's new-look cars suit his driving style. The problem, you see, was

Kimi loathes PR duties, but last year he was not able to do all his talking on the track.

qualifying, as he struggled to get the heat he required into his tyres for that lap of glory. In race trim, though, he was right on it. By then, though, it was too late and he

didn't always seem to be that interested, simply collecting the fastest lap as if to show what could have been.

TRACK NOTES

Nationality:	FINNISH
Born:	17 OCTOBER, 1979, ESPOO, FINLAND
Website:	www.kimiraikkonen.com
Teams:	SAUBER 2001, McLAREN 2002-2006, FERRARI 2007-2009

CAREER RECORD

First Grand Prix:	2001 AUSTRALIAN GP
Grand Prix starts:	140
Grand Prix wins:	17
	2003 Malaysian GP, 2004 Belgian GP, 2005 Spanish GP, Monaco GP, Canadian GP, Hungarian GP, Turkish GP, Belgian GP, Japanese GP, 2007 Australian GP, French GP, British GP, Belgian GP, Chinese GP, Brazilian GP, 2008 Malaysian GP, Spanish GP
Poles:	16
Fastest laps:	35
Points:	521
Honours:	2007 FORMULA ONE WORLD CHAMPION, 2005 & 2003 FORMULA ONE RUNNER-UP, 2000 BRITISH FORMULA RENAULT CHAMPION, 1999 BRITISH FORMULA RENAULT WINTER SERIES CHAMPION, 1998 EUROPEAN SUPER A KART RUNNER-UP & FINNISH KART CHAMPION & NORDIC KART CHAMPION

RISING LIKE A ROCKET

No driver has ever moved from karts to Formula One in as few races as Kimi did. It took him just 23. This was astonishing, but it justified the faith placed in him by former racer Steve Robertson who had been tipped off to take a look at him when he was starring in karts in 1998, cleaning up in Scandinavia and finishing up as runner-up in the European championship. Robertson placed him on a management contract on the spot. That the leap from karts to F1 was something that he took in his stride revealed that he was a driver blessed with outstanding talent. That he shone when he joined Sauber for 2001 was even more surprising as he had driven only in Formula Renault, not even Formula Three. In the points on his debut, Kimi landed a drive with McLaren for 2003 and was runner-up to Michael Schumacher, as he was in 2005. It took a move to Ferrari to yield a last-gasp world title in 2007.

BMW SAUBER

BMW Sauber continued its remarkable progress in 2008 by taking its first win, and cementing its place as the third best team behind Ferrari and McLaren. Kept in the hunt by remarkable reliability, it knows that it still has speed to find.

Robert Kubica turned into BMW Sauber's lead driver and wants a title.

Even casual study of last season's World Championship results reveals that BMW Sauber achieved close to its maximum potential in being ranked third overall, while Ferrari and McLaren squandered opportunities and fell far below their own potential. This is not to deride the Swiss-German team. Far from it, because the melding of BMW's corporate might and no little motorsport expertise with the Sauber team at its base in Hinwil, Switzerland has borne fruit in less time than other manufacturers have taken to achieve considerably less. That maiden victory at the Canadian GP last June was more than the likes of Toyota have achieved and, unlike Honda, its success was bolstered by a string of strong results rather than being a flash in the pan. And it's clear that there's more to come.

BMW Sauber now has magnificent design facilities, a clear grasp of how to use Computational Fluid Dynamics to good effect and a highly-rated wind tunnel. Its confidence has grown with this evolution, too, and the team is now a leader rather than a follower in many areas of aerodynamics. This is why it has a good chance of producing the best interpretation of the new-for-2009 aerodynamic rules.

TEAM VIPS

MARIO THEISSEN

A degree in engineering set Mario fair and his first job was in BMW's engine calculation department. He worked in various branches of BMW in the early 1990s, then set up BMW's technology office in the USA before being appointed BMW motorsport director jointly with Gerhard Berger in 1999. On becoming the main man in 2003, he guided BMW away from its partnership with Williams and forged the partnership with Sauber to give BMW its very own team.

WILLY RAMPF

This genial German has a long history with BMW. Having studied engineering in Munich, his first job was with that city's manufacturer: BMW. He worked as a test engineer for 15 years until moving to Formula One with Sauber in 1994, working as a race engineer. After a return to BMW to oversee its motorcycle involvement in the Paris-Dakar Rally, Willy rejoined Sauber, taking over as its technical director, and so was reunited again with BMW when it took the team over.

Charges have been levelled that this is a team that starts each campaign with a bang and then fails to progress at the same pace as its principal rivals, thus slipping back down the order through the season. This looked to be happening again in 2008 and the feisty Robert Kubica let the management know that he wasn't happy with the situation. At the time, as he was an outside bet for the drivers' title and, for the time being, didn't give a damn about BMW Sauber's 2009 chances. Here was the team's opportunity, he said, as well as his, and they had to grab it.

As results show, BMW Sauber came up short, but it was close enough to the ultimate pace to go away with a far clearer idea of how it might be able to reduce the gap in future, learning that it's not just a chase for more and more downforce, but more the search for the right sort of downforce that offers the drivers the balance that they need to win races.

In a team in which egos are kept well in check and success happily attributed to 'the people back at base', there is a lack of star names, but that suits the team ethos. The main change for 2009 is that technical director Willy Rampf changed his role at the end of last season to become technical co-ordinator, thus lightening his workload and ensuring that he has time to take even more of an overview of the whole campaign for further victories, with all business operations and line management duties being passed on to former project manager Walter Riedl.

Kubica, who had a mathematical chance of winning the drivers' title until the penultimate round, stays on and is now the undisputed team leader. It's not just his spectacular speed but his drive, the push, the focus that no champion is without.

Nick Heidfeld stays on too, but his inability to qualify as well as he should certainly harmed his chances and it is said that it took team chief Mario Theissen defending him to the BMW board that kept this great little racer on board.

FOR THE RECORD

Country of origin:	Switzerland
Team base:	Hinwil, Switzerland
Telephone:	(41) 44 937 9000
Website:	www.bmw-sauber-f1.com
Active in Formula One:	From 1993 (as Sauber)
Grands Prix contested:	270
Wins:	1
Pole positions:	1
Fastest laps:	2

2008 DRIVERS & RESULTS

Driver	Nationality	Races	Wins	Pts	Pos
Nick Heidfeld	German	18	-	60	6th
Robert Kubica	Polish	18	1	75	4th

THE TEAM

Team principal:	Mario Theissen
Technical co-ordinator:	Willy Rampf
Chief designer:	Christoph Zimmerman
Head of powertrain:	Markus Duesman
Project manager:	Walter Riedl
Head of aerodynamics:	Willem Toet
Head of track engineering:	Mike Krack
Team manager:	Beat Zehnder
Test driver:	tba
Chassis:	F1.09
Engine:	BMW V8
Tyres:	Bridgestone

Mario Theissen and Willy Rampf enjoyed that winning feeling in 2008.

ROBERT KUBICA

Robert scored his first grand prix win last year, but he did more than that as his performances were so uniformly excellent and mistake-free that many thought him a more worthy candidate to be champion than Lewis Hamilton or Felipe Massa.

Think about that for a moment: the experts rated Robert more highly than the two world title protagonists, the drivers armed with cars from top teams Ferrari and McLaren. That he kept himself in the title race until an out-of-sorts run in qualifying at the Chinese GP, the penultimate race, spoke volumes for his efforts.

Don't forget, too, that Robert showed more than awesome speed and accuracy out on the track. Unhappy that BMW Sauber's thoughts appeared to be turning more to developing its car for 2009 rather than keeping on with trying to match Ferrari and McLaren, he also showed impressive determination off it. If the team into which BMW has pumped so much investment ever wants to go for a title, then why not have a shot at this one he said. Yes, it was ahead of their gameplan, but it was too good a chance to miss. They must press on he said, and it's not often that a driver in only his second full season is so forceful with his employers.

Robert has won a GP and now expects the team to help him challenge for the title.

Look at the Pole's results and it's clear that he was getting the most out of the F1.08 in the first half of the year. That this moved up a gear when Hamilton crashed in the pit lane of the Canadian GP was a bonus, but he didn't put a wheel wrong and the way the team treated him that day showed how it saw him rather than the established Nick Heidfeld as its best bet.

Robert's excellence in qualifying was the key to him winning the intra-team battle, but it was his all-round belligerence and spark that put his name onto Ferrari's shopping list.

TRACK NOTES

Nationality:	POLISH
Born:	7 DECEMBER 1984, KRACOW, POLAND
Website:	www.kubica.pl
Teams:	BMW SAUBER 2006-2009

CAREER RECORD	
First Grand Prix:	2006 HUNGARIAN GP
Grand Prix starts:	40
Grand Prix wins:	1
	2008 Canadian GP
Poles:	1
Fastest laps:	0
Points:	120
Honours:	2005 WORLD SERIES BY RENAULT CHAMPION, 1999 GERMAN & ITALIAN KARTING CHAMPION, 1999 MONACO KART CUP WINNER, 1998 ITALIAN KARTING CHAMPION, 1998 MONACO KART CUP WINNER, 1997 POLISH KARTING CHAMPION

THE DRIVER HAMILTON FEARED

It takes a lot for a driver to offer praise to a rival, and it means even more if that praise comes from Lewis Hamilton. He and Robert had raced each other in karting, with Lewis singling the Pole out as his most feared rival. That Robert was still rising up racing's ladder is due only to his family's determination and this included Robert moving to Italy to race. Sacrifices were made and Renault snapped him up for Formula Renault and he was runner-up in the 2002 Italian series. Just as his momentum was picking up again, in European Formula Three, he broke an arm and missed much of the season. But he was a race winner before the year was out. Graduating to the World Series by Renault for 2005, Robert took the title and BMW slipped him into a race seat when it tired of Jacques Villeneuve in mid-2006. He was on the podium in only his third race and then shone in 2007, even surviving a life-threatening shunt in Canada.

NICK HEIDFELD

You had to feel for Nick when BMW Sauber scored its first win last season and he helped his team-mate Robert Kubica to achieve it. Add to that, Kubica was generally faster and Nick had to change his style. Now he must deliver, or else...

Here's a question: did Nick grow a beard in 2008 so that he had something to hide behind? At times, you felt that he did and no one would have blamed him.

Nick is a driver who has a great career record, but it lacks one thing: a grand prix win. With all the experience gained from nine years in Formula One, and the familiarity of six years with the team that is now BMW Sauber, he ought to be in a position to become a winner. However, the fact that Kubica gave the team its only win shouldn't freak Nick out too much as it was a race driven by events rather than form. What got to him was the fact that Kubica was getting far more out of the car, outqualifying him three to one. This was mainly down to Nick's less aggressive driving style preventing him from getting heat into the tyres to nail a flying lap.

There were a trio of second place finishes, at the Melbourne season-opener, at Montreal (spoiled by Kubica finishing first) and at Spa-Francorchamps when Lewis Hamilton was given his 25s penalty, and

Nick was always quick in races but needs to improve his qualifying to match Kubica.

that's not a bad tally in a year when the Ferraris and McLarens ought to have filled the top four places if they didn't trip up.

Nick did close the gap on Kubica by season's end. In fact, he trounced him

in qualifying in Shanghai, but the key to staying with a team that may be in a position to give him that maiden victory, hinges on how the pair compare in the season ahead. Then perhaps he can stop hiding behind that beard.

TRACK NOTES

Nationality:	GERMAN
Born:	10 MAY, 1977, MOENCHENGLADBACH, GERMANY
Website:	www.nickheidfeld.de
Teams:	PROST 2000, SAUBER 2001-2003, JORDAN 2004, WILLIAMS 2005, BMW SAUBER 2006-2009

CAREER RECORD

First Grand Prix:	2000 AUSTRALIAN GP
Grand Prix starts:	152
Grand Prix wins:	0
Poles:	1
Fastest laps:	2
Points:	200
Honours:	1999 FORMULA 3000 CHAMPION, 1998 FORMULA 3000 RUNNER-UP, 1997 GERMAN FORMULA THREE CHAMPION, 1995 GERMAN FORMULA FORD RUNNER-UP, 1994 GERMAN FF1600 CHAMPION

HELPED ALONG THE WAY

Before he could grow a beard, Nick was the baby-faced assassin, scything through Germany's junior formulae. Formula Ford title, check. Formula Three title, check. And so to Formula 3000 where he fought with Juan Pablo Montoya then won the title at his second attempt. With two years of Formula One testing under his belt thanks to longtime backers Mercedes, a race seat was next, but as there were no seats open at McLaren, Nick joined Prost for 2000. Neither he nor team-mate Jean Alesi managed to score, but a move to Sauber in 2001 brought his first podium, for third in Brazil and he ranked eighth. Progress was hard, and he looked out of a drive after spending 2004 with Jordan, but BMW wanted a German at Williams so he went there, before BMW took him back to Sauber (now BMW Sauber) for 2006 and he had his best season in 2007, ranking fifth overall.

RENAULT

With Fernando Alonso under contract until the end of the 2010 World Championship, Renault can now move forward sure in the fact that if it produces a car capable of winning it will be taking home the victory laurels.

Renault's principal asset in 2009 will again be feisty Fernando Alonso.

Whatever happened on the track last year, race wins or not, there was talk that this French manufacturer would pull the plug, scrap its Formula One programme. This was frequently refuted, even by Renault Chief Executive Carlos Ghosn, but had it happened it would have sent a shockwave through the World Championship, rocked it to its core, as Renault has been such a key ingredient over the years both as a team entrant and as an engine supplier. Good grief, its racing involvement goes all the way back to 1906 when Renault won the first ever grand prix.

This didn't come to pass, but certain Formula One journalists even hinted that they thought that Renault's late-season surge in competitiveness was down to something sinister, an allowance to keep Renault on board. That was an insult to the team's integrity and to the sheer diligence of the engineering and design teams. And also to the considerable dynamic force that is Fernando Alonso.

The fact that Alonso re-signed last November through to the end of the 2010 season is all the proof that is needed that the Renault team will be with us for a while yet.

Renault started to show good form from mid-season last year, but it certainly took the fluke of optimal deployment of the safety car at the Singapore GP to turn

TEAM VIPS

FLAVIO BRIATORE
Flamboyant Flavio continues to pretend that he doesn't like motor racing, and it's true that he came to it in 1989 only at the behest of the Benetton family to run its team after he'd successfully established Benetton's clothing brand in the USA. More aware than his dyed-in-the-wool racer contemporaries that Formula One must entertain, he has also scored considerable success, with two drivers' titles for Michael Schumacher and then a pair for Fernando Alonso when the team metamorphosed to Renault.

PAT SYMONDS
A designer of Formula Ford cars as long ago as 1976, Pat is the person to ask if you want a no-nonsense answer. He's witty too, and has seen it all over the years since reaching Formula One with Toleman in 1982. After being director of engineering on Reynard's aborted Formula One bid, Pat engineered Michael Schumacher to two titles with Benetton and became technical director, then executive director of engineering when the team became Renault.

the team into a winning force again for the first time since Alonso left there at the end of 2006 to go and join McLaren.

One thing that will be different in 2009 is that the flamboyant team figurehead, Flavio Briatore, won't be so much in evidence. He is tipped to appoint former GP2 chief Bruno Michel to conduct many of his day-to-day management duties and will thus be free to spend more of his time giving direction to his football club, Queens Park Rangers. If the wins flow, though, expect Flavio to be there for the victory celebrations, his favourite part of a sport he once famously boasted of not understanding.

Most importantly, executive director of engineering Pat Symonds will continue to be at the grands prix, as he talks more sense than probably anyone the length of the pit lane. For example, he proposed that all teams' fuel loads are published before the start of races. Just think how that would improve the show. He also wanted to award points right the way down the order, so you can be sure that he is prepared to think outside the box to spread Formula One's popularity.

Renault is like that, a sensible team that is prepared to try new things, staffed by good people such as Bob Bell, Tim Densham and Alan Permane. Sadly, they lost Dino Toso to cancer last summer, and his position as director of aerodynamic technology was taken over last April by Dirk de Beer, and his impact was clear as Renault improved strongly in the final races.

However, above all things, the fact that Alonso has signed not only for 2009 but 2010 as well will drive the team forward, for he is a driver who simply never backs off and will obviously be motivated to try and topple both Lewis Hamilton and his former team McLaren.

Nelson Piquet Jr has been kept on for a second season and will have to show improved form if he is to be much of a help to the team's points tally.

FOR THE RECORD

Country of origin:	England
Team base:	Enstone, England
Telephone:	(44) 01608 678000
Website:	www.ing-renaultf1.com
Active in Formula One:	From 1977-85 and from 2002
Grands Prix contested:	246*
Wins:	35
Pole positions:	49
Fastest laps:	27

* NOTE THAT THESE FIGURES DO NOT INCLUDE THE 238 RACES THE TEAM RAN AS BENETTON

2008 DRIVERS & RESULTS

Driver	Nationality	Races	Wins	Pts	Pos
Fernando Alonso	Spanish	18	2	61	5th
Nelson Piquet Jr	Brazilian	18	-	19	12th

THE TEAM

President:	Bernard Rey
Managing director:	Flavio Briatore
Deputy managing director (engine):	Rob White
Deputy managing director (support operations):	Andre Laine
Technical director:	Bob Bell
Executive director of engineering:	Pat Symonds
Deputy technical director:	James Allison
Head of trackside operations:	Denis Chevrier
Chief designer:	Tim Densham
Chief engineer:	Alan Permane
Team manager:	Steve Nielsen
Test drivers:	tba
Chassis:	Renault R29
Engine:	Renault V8
Tyres:	Bridgestone

Pat Symonds does the common sense, Flavio Briatore the profile.

FERNANDO ALONSO

Fernando left McLaren branded as petulant and worse, then raced through most of 2008 deep in the midfield pack, but he never gave up and drove every lap as if it was his last, ending up with two grand prix wins. There may be more this year.

Fernando's behaviour in 2007 as he fell out of love with Lewis Hamilton and McLaren was unattractive. Even those who had admired his talent saw him in a new light. Luckily, he returned to the only team that understood him: Renault. However, he found it a very different proposition to when he left just 12 months earlier. Less competitive, that's for sure.

The important thing was that Fernando dug in and as the year advanced and the Renault became more competitive, his input was rewarded, The first of his two wins, in Singapore, was a fluke, presented to him by the fortuitous timing of the safety car. Ironically, the form he'd shown until he'd had a mechanical problem in qualifying had been pace-setting. So it was he started 15th not first and set out with a bizarre tactic in the hope of taking a point or two and it came to him.

To then go and win, on merit, in Japan was a different proposition, although the Ferraris and McLarens did their best to eliminate themselves on race day.

Fernando grew up in 2008, and the way that he channelled his aggression was impressive.

What Fernando did to get himself back into his critics' good books was to attack, attack, attack. Few of his rivals can match his intensity and Fernando said that if he takes one thing into 2009, it's that he has learned how to maximise his car for qualifying, letting it all follow from there.

Still, this most competitive of men must wonder what he could have achieved if he had not burnt his bridges with McLaren.

TRACK NOTES

Nationality:	SPANISH
Born:	29 JULY, 1981, OVIEDO, SPAIN
Website:	www.fernandoalonso.com
Teams:	MINARDI 2001, RENAULT 2003-2006, McLAREN 2007, RENAULT 2008-2009

CAREER RECORD

First Grand Prix:	2001 AUSTRALIAN GP
Grand Prix starts:	123
Grand Prix wins:	21
	2003 Hungarian GP, 2005 Malaysian GP, Bahrain GP, San Marino GP, European GP, French GP, German GP, Chinese GP, 2006 Bahrain GP, Australian GP, Spanish GP, Monaco GP, British GP, Canadian GP, Japanese GP, 2007 Malaysian GP, Monaco GP, European GP, Italian GP, 2008 Singapore GP, Japanese GP
Poles:	16
Fastest laps:	11
Points:	641
Honours:	2005 & 2006 FORMULA ONE WORLD CHAMPION, 1999 FORMULA NISSAN CHAMPION, 1997 ITALIAN & SPANISH KART CHAMPION, 1996 WORLD & SPANISH KART CHAMPION

A LOSER AT POLITICS

Fernando is one of the top three drivers, and this will come as no surprise to anyone who witnessed his talents in karting. He was World Champion in 1996 and when he was old enough to race cars clinched the Formula Nissan title. Stepping up to Formula 3000, he went faster with every round before blitzing his rivals at the toughest track: Spa-Francorchamps. Minardi snapped him up for 2001. More useful was his year as Renault test driver in 2002. Racing for Renault in 2003, he became the youngest grand prix winner, just after his 22nd birthday. Fernando broke another record in 2005 when he became the youngest champion. After another title in 2006, it was off to McLaren and it was here that he lost the plot, being out-psyched by rookie Lewis Hamilton and quitting the team, which backfired as he had to return to less competitive Renault.

NELSON PIQUET JR

Nelson Piquet Jr led a grand prix last year, the German GP at Hockenheim, but this was in stark contrast to much of his form and many were surprised that he was retained for 2009. So, now is his chance to prove his many critics wrong.

When Nelson Piquet Jr found himself all at sea in the first half of the 2008 World Championship, many called for him to be dropped from the team as early as May, but his subsequent improvement as he began racing on circuits he knew was sufficient for him to be given a second chance. He finally scored his first points at his eighth attempt by finishing seventh in the French GP and went on to score 19 points overall.

Nelsinho's advance came hand in hand with the Renault R28 becoming easier to drive as it was sorted and although he led the German GP largely due to the timing of a safety car deployment and raced on to finish an astounding second, his best race was certainly his run to fourth place in the Japanese GP. Between these events, though, there were still too many mistakes, although it could be added that Nelson's Singapore GP slip-up was worth its weight in gold, as it handed the race to team-mate Fernando Alonso...

Nelsinho knows that he was lucky to be kept on and must make the most of this chance.

When the going got tough, there was talk that test driver Lucas di Grassi, who was in storming form in GP2, might be promoted in his stead. Di Grassi's name came up again at the end of the season, proof that Renault is keen on having a Brazilian in its second car for marketing reasons. However, the experience Nelsinho had gained was too much just to discard, and so he stays, for this season at least.

What Renault really needs to see from Nelsinho is consistent form and, always a failing of Nelsinho's, they need to see more aggression. His background has guided him to F1 rather than a burning inner desire, and this ingredient could prove vital and prevent him becoming an Formula One star

TRACK NOTES

Nationality:	BRAZILIAN
Born:	25 JULY, 1984, HEIDELBERG, GERMANY
Website:	www.piquetsports.com.br
Teams:	2008-2009 RENAULT

CAREER RECORD

First Grand Prix:	2008 AUSTRALIAN GP
Grand Prix starts:	18
Grand Prix wins:	0
Poles:	0
Fastest laps:	0
Points:	19
Honours:	2006 GP2 RUNNER-UP, 2004 BRITISH FORMULA THREE CHAMPION, 2002 SOUTH AMERICAN FORMULA THREE CHAMPION

HAVING TO TRY THAT LITTLE BIT HARDER

It was inevitable that Nelson Jr would be put onto a kart as soon as he was old enough to drive one. After all, almost all racing drivers do that for their offspring rather than suggesting a career as a family doctor might be a rather better option. As a three-time world champion who seemed addicted to the thrill of racing, Nelson Sr expected it more than most and not only bankrolled Nelson Jr's karting career and his move to car racing in 2001, but made sure that he had the very best of equipment and tested whenever possible. The fruits were the South American Formula Three title in his first full season and the British Formula Three crown two years later. You couldn't do this without talent, but rivals were jealous about the budget he enjoyed. They had to bite their lips, though, when Nelson Jr finished as runner-up to Lewis Hamilton in GP2 in 2006. Snapped up as Renault's test driver for 2007, he had his foot in Formula One's door and the mileage he covered in testing then was invaluable.

TOYOTA

This Japanese giant claimed to have limited ambitions when it hit Formula One in 2002, favouring a step-by-step approach. By now, though, it would have expected to be race winners if not championship challengers, but it is getting there slowly.

Steady progress by Toyota hints that Jarno Trulli might yet win again.

There were positive signs last year that Toyota is finally going places, finally showing signs that the car in front might really be a Toyota, to bastardise one of their advertising campaigns. After years of underachievement and, to a degree, anonymity, Toyota began to be seen and started to challenge in 2008, putting two poor championship campaigns in 2006 and 2007 behind them.

There were positive signs from the start of last season, with fourth place for Jarno Trulli at the second round, in Malaysia, and sixth place next time out, in Bahrain. But, and this is a sign of the distance that Toyota still needs to travel on the design front, it was left behind when

all of the teams introduced new aerodynamic packages for the Spanish GP and pulled clear of Toyota again.

Toyota then displayed a fighting spirit that has been missing before and technical chief Pascal Vasselon introduced new front and rear wings for the French GP and they worked so well that Trulli started third and finished third. It was a breakthrough, and at this point that the team believed that it ought to be able to finish the year fourth overall. It would have done so, too, had not Renault awoken from its slumbers and outstripped it with its Singapore-inspired flurry.

The other highlight of the

year was the Hungarian GP when the TF108's preference for circuits of a more twisting nature was made plain. Not only did Glock bounce back from his major accident in the German GP, but he ended the race in second place. Had Trulli not constantly got stuck behind slower cars that afternoon, he'd have scored well there too. Also, had Trulli not been speared at the first corner of the Chinese GP by Sebastien Bourdais, a decent result was on the cards there as well.

The driver line-up stays the same for 2009, with Trulli back for a fifth season and Glock staying for a second. Give Trulli a competitive car and he will make it fly, although cruel fortune tends to scupper more of his best runs than it does to any other driver.

Glock also catches the eye and it's clear that a little internal competition works for both as they push each other on to greater things. Toyota are fortunate too that they appear to get on really well when out of the cockpit and work towards a common cause, that certainly wasn't the case when Trulli was paired with Ralf Schumacher.

One individual who will have helped the team and drivers to see the wood from the trees is the hugely experienced Frank Dernie who joined in April in the role of senior advisor.

On the personnel front, team manager Richard Cregan has left the team, heading off to join the organizers of this year's new grand prix, in Abu Dhabi.

There were rumours in circulation last January that Toyota might quit Formula One and then again last October that they might prefer to focus on trying to win the Le Mans 24 Hour sports car race, angered by the FIA's suggestion of the use of standard engines, but team president John Howett scotched those rumours, describing them as malicious. You can't help feeling that with the progress made through 2008 that the thought is far from their minds and that pulling out now would be an admission of failure.

Tadashi Yamashina is hoping to guide Toyota to wins in 2009.

FOR THE RECORD

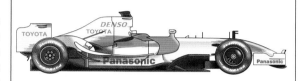

Country of origin:	Germany
Team base:	Cologne, Germany
Telephone:	(49) 2234 1823444
Website:	www.toyota-f1.com
Active in Formula One:	From 2002
Grands Prix contested:	123
Wins:	0
Pole positions:	2
Fastest laps:	1

2008 DRIVERS & RESULTS

Driver	Nationality	Races	Wins	Pts	Pos
Timo Glock	German	18	-	25	10th
Jarno Trulli	Italian	18	-	31	9th

THE TEAM

Chairman & team principal:	Tadashi Yamashina
President:	John Howett
Executive vice-president:	Yoshiaki Kinoshita
General manager, engine:	Luca Marmorini
General manager, chassis:	Pascal Vasselon
Technical co-ordinator:	Noritoshi Arai
Chief engineer:	Dieter Gass
Head of aerodynamics:	Mark Gillan
Team manager:	tba
Test driver:	Kamui Kobayashi
Chassis:	Toyota TF109
Engine:	Toyota V8
Tyres:	Bridgestone

JARNO TRULLI

This long-serving Italian gave his all in 2008 and Toyota offered him ever-better machinery with which to do so. Many firmly believe that if Toyota can get its new car right, to the new rules, he could yet score that second grand prix win.

This charismatic Italian driver is seen by mercurial as some, something of an enigma by others. One glance at his racing pedigree is enough to show that he has always been an exceptional talent. After all, no one becomes World Kart Champion without being the best of the best. Just ask Fernando Alonso. And yet, late last year, Jarno was still being defensive about his Formula One record that stretches back to 1997, saying that his critics must be blind. It's easy to back his view. After all, anyone who can lead a grand prix in a Prost must be exceptional...

All Jarno needs is a winning chassis, and he's only had one once, in 2004, when he won at Monaco and his team-mate Alonso failed to win all year, reversing their roles from the previous year. However, he was eased out of Renault before that year was out and has raced for midfielders Toyota ever since. Of course, Jarno would have had a car capable of winning had he been kept on by Renault, as Alonso stayed on

Jarno reached the podium at the French GP but wants to return to the top step in 2009.

and won two straight world titles in 2005 and 2006.

Yet, Toyota has every chance of continuing to progress in 2009, building on a strong end to last year's campaign. Any year when the technical regulations are given a major shake-up offers the chance for the playing field to be level, albeit briefly, although the usual teams usually settle back at the top. If Toyota can excel, then Jarno will finally have the chance to silence his critics and show that he can race every bit as well as he can qualify.

TRACK NOTES

Nationality:	ITALIAN
Born:	13 JULY, 1974, PESCARA, ITALY
Website:	www.jarnotrulli.com
Teams:	MINARDI
1997, PROST 1997-1999, JORDAN 2000-2001, RENAULT 2002-2004, TOYOTA 2005-2009	

CAREER RECORD

First Grand Prix:	1997 AUSTRALIAN GP
Grand Prix starts:	202
Grand Prix wins:	1
	2004 Monaco GP
Poles:	3
Fastest laps:	0
Points:	214
Honours:	1996 GERMAN FORMULA THREE CHAMPION, 1995 WORLD & ITALIAN KARTING CHAMPION, 1994 EUROPEAN & NORTH AMERICAN KARTING CHAMPION, 1991 WORLD KARTING CHAMPION

MISTER KARTING BIG SHOT

Some drivers take a while to get going, but Jarno wasn't one of those, landing the world karting title when he was 17 and another four years later in a more powerful category. Using his eye for talent, Flavio Briatore put Jarno directly into Formula Three midway through 1995, skipping the junior classes. Jarno was immediately quick, beating Ralf Schumacher in the final two German championship rounds. Entered for a full season in 1996, Jarno became champion, with Nick Heidfeld third. With his year and a half in cars added to his karting, he felt he was ready for Formula One. Cocky? Yes, but he was immediately strong for Minardi on joining them for 1997 and he even led the Austrian GP after being transferred to Prost. Since then, no one can deny Jarno his speed in qualifying, but his race results haven't been as good, his win for Renault at Monaco in 2004 aside, as expected. He has never driven for a truly top team, though.

TIMO GLOCK

They say that you don't get two chances in life, but Timo is proof that you can and is making the most of his second shot at Formula One, with his reputation soaring after an increasingly strong first full season with Toyota. Now he wants race wins.

It is also said that what doesn't break you can make you stronger and this combative German proved that to be true. Consider the situation: Toyota had brought him back to Formula One three and a half years after he had four outings for the team that was then Jordan. He'd finished seventh on his debut in 2004, but that wasn't seen as enough for him to be kept on. The opening half of the 2008 campaign had produced one point-scoring drive, to fourth place in the topsy-turvy Canadian GP. By comparison, team-mate Jarno Trulli had scored six times. Then came the German GP and Glock ran wide out of the final corner and his car snapped away from under him and he slammed into the pit wall. It was a big one, but he was hauled out. Battered and bruised he most certainly was, but bowed he was not, so he turned up ready to race next time out in Hungary, as you'd expect from someone who had just been given a contract extension, and he raced to a sensational second place.

Timo grew stronger with almost every race through 2008 and is in Formula One to stay.

If the paddock hadn't been sold on him before, as he'd been somewhat inconsistent, they most certainly were now, and Timo's currency seemed to rise with almost every race thereafter, perhaps corresponding with a gain in form by Toyota. Fourth place in the bizarre Singapore GP also boosted Timo's reputation.

So, it's small wonder that Timo was signed up to stay for a second year with the Cologne-based team and he seems to be the level-headed sort of character who listens to his engineer's advice in particular and consequently improves with experience. Perhaps the fact that he had it once and had to let it go has made him all the more determined to grasp this opportunity with both hands.

TRACK NOTES

Nationality:	GERMAN
Born:	18 MARCH, 1982, LINDENFELS, GERMANY
Website:	www.timo-glock.de
Teams:	JORDAN 2004, TOYOTA 2008-2009

CAREER RECORD

First Grand Prix:	2004 CANADIAN GP
Grand Prix starts:	22
Grand Prix wins:	0
Poles:	0
Fastest laps:	0
Points:	27
Honours:	2007 GP2 CHAMPION, 2001 GERMAN FORMULA BMW CHAMPION, 2000 GERMAN FORMULA BMW JUNIOR CHAMPION

SUCCESS AT THE SECOND BITE

Britain and Germany offer the most competitive training grounds for aspiring racing drivers and Timo signalled his talents by winning a title in his first year out of karts. This was in Formula BMW Junior. He then won the Formula BMW series the following year. Ranking third in German Formula Three in 2002 confirmed Timo as one to watch, with 2003 yielding fifth place in the European Formula Three championship. Then came 2004 when he was promoted from his test driving role with the Jordan Formula One team to a race seat as a replacement for Giorgio Pantano. Seventh on his debut in Canada was remarkable, but he didn't keep the ride and ended up in ChampCar in 2005. He was top rookie and nearly won one round, but Formula One was still Timo's aim so he opted to contest GP2 in 2006, but couldn't keep Lewis Hamilton from the crown and so had a second crack at it in 2007, duly becoming champion.

TORO ROSSO

When Minardi was Minardi, no one expected points, let alone wins. Yet, after Minardi became Toro Rosso, that started to change. Then Sebastian Vettel raised the team's sights with victory last year, but what does 2009 hold in store?

Toro Rosso climbed to the front of the midfield and aims to stay there.

First up, it's only fair to point out that the budget enjoyed by the Toro Rosso team is far in excess of the one on which the old team – Minardi – would scrape by, as Red Bull has poured considerable money into the team. Also, the use of a chassis that was or was not, according to whom you spoke, the same as the Adrian Newey-designed Red Bull RB4 was certainly not a hindrance. Sure, the mating of this with a Ferrari V8 rather than the Renault engine used by Red Bull Racing meant that there were differences, but both came from Red Bull Technology and so that part-explained the fact that Scuderia Toro Rosso scored its first win last year.

And, what a win. It came in the wet at Monza after Toro Rosso had both drivers finish in the points in fifth and seventh at the Belgian GP, but it was certainly no fluke as Sebastian Vettel had qualified on pole position and led almost as he pleased from there. This wasn't a win created from nowhere by the race order being turned on its head by the incursion of the safety car. To see the way Vettel harried Felipe Massa for the lead of the Brazilian GP, albeit with a lighter fuel load, and then took on and outran Lewis Hamilton's McLaren was eye-opening and a major tribute not only to the machinery at his disposal but also the tactical nous of Franz Tost, Giorgio Ascanelli and the crew.

Sebastien Bourdais seemed to take a while to come to the boil, but his performances in the second half of the season were far better than the results that he collected.

What was noticeable and was very different to what happened in the team's Minardi days is that the team evolved its chassis through the year. In fact, the STR03 actually gained on the opposition through 2008, with Giorgio Ascanelli and his crew loving it as they would get both cars into the final qualifying session in the season's closing races, meaning that points were theirs to lose rather than simply something to which to aspire.

The success and the fact that Toro Rosso was able to move up to sixth in the teams' rankings gave the team not only kudos but increased value, and this was not something to be sniffed at as team owners Dietrich Mateschitz and Gerhard Berger had been looking to sell the team.

Ambitious Ultimate Motorsport had been looking to take a stake in the team, but the matter isn't straightforward as the team knows that it will have to be a full constructor in 2010, building its own car rather than using a customer chassis. In fact, that's why it's for sale, as the associated bills are clearly going to be rather larger.

With glory boy Vettel being promoted to Red Bull's senior team alongside Mark Webber, the 2009 Scuderia Toro Rosso line-up will be Takuma Sato and Sebastien Buemi, so the Italian team has lost its cutting edge, but that is not to say that it won't be in among the points on a regular basis, showing just how far this team has come since its decades as Minardi.

FOR THE RECORD

Country of origin:	Italy
Team base:	Faenza, Italy
Telephone:	(39) 546 696111
Website:	www.scuderiatorosso.com
Active in Formula One:	From 1985 (as Minardi until 2006)
Grands Prix contested:	376
Wins:	1
Pole positions:	1
Fastest laps:	0

2008 DRIVERS & RESULTS

Driver	Nationality	Races	Wins	Pts	Pos
Sebastien Bourdais	French	18	-	4	17th
Sebastian Vettel	German	18	1	35	8th

THE TEAM

Team owners:	Dietrich Mateschitz & Gerhard Berger
Team principal:	Franz Tost
Technical director:	Giorgio Ascanelli
Team manager:	Gianfranco Fantuzzi
Chief designer:	Alex Hitzinger (Red Bull Technology)
Chief engineer:	Laurent Mekies
Technical co-ordinator:	Sandro Parrini
Test driver:	tba
Chassis:	Scuderia Toro Rosso STR04
Engine:	Ferrari V8
Tyres:	Bridgestone

Berger, congratulating Vettel, will forever dream of this moment.

TAKUMA SATO

The smile is back. Takuma thought his Formula One career might be over when Super Aguri folded last spring, but a show of serious pace in tests for Toro Rosso has him back where he belongs and he'll give everything for this second chance.

Scuderia Toro Rosso stated that for 2009 it had a seat open for a young gun and another for an experienced hand. It was for the latter seat that 32-year-old Takuma was considered and tested late last year. Topping the timesheets on the opening day of post-season testing at Barcelona last November, ahead of 16 other drivers, was just what Takuma had to do.

Toro Rosso's backer, Red Bull, were also no doubt aware of Takuma's popularity in Japan and fully attuned to the impact he might help its energy drink enjoy on the lucrative Japanese market.

So it is that Takuma is back in Formula One, just when it looked as though all of his options had dried up, that he'd had his shot and now it was the turn of younger drivers. This is a notable achievement, as his 93 grand prix starts include just one visit to a podium, and that at the 2004 US GP for which only six cars started. However, Takuma

Takuma Sato proved he deserved another chance by topping the timesheets in testing.

has never really enjoyed a top-flight car and is acknowledged as being a good little racer. In fact, his attacking form in last year's Super Aguri in the first four

races before the plug was pulled on the team was impressive, and he clearly loves a scrap, being one of the most exciting drivers to watch on the opening lap of any grand prix as he tries to pass faster cars while they're all bunched at close quarters. So, welcome back Takuma. Welcome back to Formula One, let's hope to a life rather further up the field for a team that ought to be around all the way to the end of the world championship.

TRACK NOTES

Nationality:	JAPANESE
Born:	28 JANUARY, 1977, TOKYO, JAPAN
Website:	www.takumasato.com
Teams:	JORDAN 2002, BAR 2003-2005, SUPER AGURI RACING 2006-2008 TORO ROSSO 2009

CAREER RECORD	
First Grand Prix:	2002 AUSTRALIAN GP
Grand Prix starts:	93
Grand Prix wins:	0
	best result: third 2004 US GP
Poles:	0
Fastest laps:	0
Points:	44
Honours:	2001 BRITISH FORMULA THREE CHAMPION

CAREER HISTORY

Takuma didn't race karts and didn't really race much in Japan before he left the comfort zone and headed for the British racing scene in 1998. He impressed from the outset, possessing a clear natural speed, and this served him well as he learned the circuits. British Formula Three champion at his second attempt in 2001, Takuma had to resist a late-season charge from his Carlin Motorsport team-mate, Anthony Davidson, so it was entertaining that they were later to be paired together again. With Jordan running Honda engines in 2002, Takuma found himself making the big leap and he didn't disgrace himself. After serving 2003 as test driver for BAR, he stepped up to its race line-up for 2004 and finished third at the widely-boycotted US GP. A poor 2005 led to him being fired, and many felt Super Aguri was formed simply to give him another vehicle. Sixth place in Canada in 2007 was a highlight, but the 2008 season was somewhat short...

SEBASTIEN BUEMI

Ladies and gentlemen, please welcome the latest shooting star to hit Formula One. Just turned 20, and with considerable racing mileage behind him, Sebastien has the speed that long time backer Red Bull craves and now is his chance to show it.

Scuderia Toro Rosso soared into the limelight last year through the exploits of Sebastian Vettel. It had already recovered its pound of flesh when he brought in the dividends with his remarkable pole position followed by a flawless victory in the rain-hit Italian GP. With this in mind, one can understand its decision to promote another Sebastien, another youngster in a hurry.

He's Swiss not German, and Sebastien not Sebastian, but like his predecessor he has climbed the racing ladder with Red Bull backing and at 20 is primed to deliver. He's not a complete novice in Formula One experience either, as he was Red Bull Racing's test driver last year and this knowledge showed itself in the first post-season test session when he was immediately second fastest.

Sebastien is a young man in love with life, full of excitement at all that's put in front of him, loving his racing and the camaraderie that it can bring. He's certainly not had to

Red Bull must believe Sebastien Buemi can drive them on to greater success in 2009.

struggle to get to where he is now and so treats it as his right, and you can't blame him. It has all happened so fast, the leap from karts to top level single-seaters, but

he has crammed a lot of racing into the past four years, all over the globe.

Some might point to the lack of a title yet in car racing, but he has been rushing through categories at a younger age than his rivals. So his runner-up position in the European Formula Three series in 2007 is all the more impressive as he was only 18 at the time. In fact, examine his career path and it's a shadow of Vettel's, and that can be no bad thing.

TRACK NOTES

Nationality	SWISS
Born	31 OCTOBER, 1988, AIGLE, SWITZERLAND
Website	www.buemi.ch
Teams	TORO ROSSO 2009

CAREER RECORD

First Grand Prix	2009 AUSTRALIAN GP
Grand Prix starts	0
Grand Prix wins	0
Poles	0
Fastest laps	0
Points	0

Honours 2008 GP2 ASIA RUNNER-UP, 2007 EUROPEAN FORMULA THREE RUNNER-UP, 2005 WORLD FINAL & GERMAN FORMULA BMW RUNNER-UP, 2002 EUROPEAN JUNIOR KART CHAMPION

IN HIS BLOOD

Sebastien was always likely to go racing as both his grandfather and great uncle did. They even built their own Formula One car, the Cegga, in the early 1960s, although it never made it to a grand prix and was used in hillclimbs. Sebastien stepped up from karts to cars in 2004, when he was 15. Very competitive in Formula BMW, ending 2005 as runner-up in the world finals, he then graduated to Formula Three for 2006, claiming the European series runner-up spot in 2007 behind Romain Grosjean when he was impressively consistent and even outscored Nico Hulkenberg. As a young man in a hurry, with sizeable support from Red Bull, he also raced in GP2, setting three fastest laps but ranking only 21st. Things went better in 2008 when Sebastien was runner-up in the Asian GP2 series then advanced to sixth in the main series, taking two wins for Team Arden. He also got in some valuable testing for Red Bull's Formula One team.

RED BULL RACING

The arrangement was that Toro Rosso was the B-team, Red Bull Racing the A-team, but this backfired and you can be sure that pride alone will dictate that status quo is restored, especially with Sebastian Vettel joining the driver line-up.

Mark Webber will be hoping that his efforts are rewarded with a top car.

Red Bull is an extraordinary global phenomenon. The sheer amount of money that this energy drink has earned its co-creator Dietrich Mateschitz is truly staggering and he has invested heavily in sport.

To start with, it was adrenaline sports, of the jumping out of a plane on a surfboard variety, or climbing sheer rock faces without a rope to cling to. That certainly got the Red Bull brand noticed. Then it was motor racing, first with backing for compatriot Gerhard Berger, then team ownership and the pinnacle of this was the Austrian's purchase of the team that was once Jaguar Racing and before that Stewart. Matters only became complicated

when Mateschitz purchased the ever strapped-for-cash Minardi team and turned that into his B-team for the 2007 season.

Equipping that with an Adrian Newey-designed chassis that was all but identical to the Red Bull RB4 was the start of a problem as it put it on to a level plain with the senior team, then beat it... Yes, that dream of a first win for Red Bull Racing will be somewhat diluted if it is ever achieved as a lot of its thunder was stolen by Scuderia Toro Rosso when it not only raced to victory on that steaming wet day at Monza last September but did so from pole position.

However, if a few feathers were ruffled in this quasi-

TEAM VIPS

DIETRICH MATESCHITZ
A man who becomes richer by the minute as his Red Bull energy drinks conquer the world, Dietrich sponsors not one but two Formula One teams. Having decided that extreme sports were the best way to promote Red Bull, he followed up his love of racing by buying what had been Jaguar Racing for 2005 and renaming it. As well as backing many rising drivers, Dietrich then joined forces with compatriot Gerhard Berger to buy Minardi, and so formed Scuderia Toro Rosso.

ADRIAN NEWEY
Lauded as Formula One's top designer, Adrian started with the Fittipaldi team in 1980. March snapped Adrian up and he designed title-winning sports cars and Indycars before penning its Formula One cars from 1987, with his aerodynamic excellence smoothing his move to Williams in 1990. Titles started flowing and McLaren signed him for 1997. Drivers' titles in 1998 and 1999 proved his worth and he stayed until 2006 when he moved on to Red Bull. Adrian also has a collection of historic racing cars that he races when he can.

internal battle, it was nothing to the way the team was viewed by the opposition, especially those teams whose cars were trailing in their wake, those who claimed the Toro Rosso STR03 was closer to being an outlawed customer car than they thought right.

To make sure that the A-team, Red Bull Racing, returns to its intended place in the pecking order, Mark Webber is joined for 2009 by last year's Toro Rosso revelation, Sebastian Vettel, who fills the seat vacated by David Coulthard who has stepped into retirement. This will ensure an interesting year ahead as Webber was the undisputed king of qualifying in the team,

as this was never Coulthard's forte. Vettel, though, can hang it out with the best of them over a single flying lap, so it will be absolutely intriguing to watch this new head-to-head which is sure to wring the best out of them both.

Red Bull Racing can be relieved that they have secured Vettel too, as there was even talk last spring that team principal Christian Horner was looking to drop Coulthard there and then to snap up Vettel in order to stop him from being pinched by rival teams BMW Sauber or Ferrari. This was something that Horner refuted and would have felt vindicated

when the Scot's wise head helped him to a podium finish in the Canadian GP.

The progress that Newey and Geoff Willis achieved last year was clear to see in the final four or five grands prix, as championship points were scored more often than not and everyone at the Milton Keynes-

based team will be hoping that Newey is able to use his famous grey matter to find the best interpretation of the new aerodynamic rules to give Red Bull Racing its best shot yet at victory. Ally this with the improved reliability that will be Willis's focus, and Red Bull might yet hit the bull's eye.

FOR THE RECORD

Country of origin:	England
Team base:	Milton Keynes, England
Telephone:	(44) 1908 279700
Website:	www.redbullracing.com
Active in Formula One:	From 1997 (as Stewart until 2000 then Jaguar Racing until 2004)
Grands Prix contested:	206
Wins:	1
Pole positions:	1
Fastest laps:	0

2008 DRIVERS & RESULTS

Driver	Nationality	Races	Wins	Pts	Pos
David Coulthard	British	18	-	8	16th
Mark Webber	Australian	18	-	21	11th

THE TEAM

Chairman:	Dietrich Mateschitz
Team principal:	Christian Horner
Chief technical officer:	Adrian Newey
Technical director:	Geoff Willis
Head of race & test engineering:	Paul Monaghan
Chief designer:	Rob Marshall
Head of aerodynamics:	Peter Prodromou
Head of R&D:	Andrew Green
Team manager:	Jonathan Wheatley
Test driver:	tba
Chassis:	Red Bull RB5
Engine:	Renault V8
Tyres:	Bridgestone

Mark Webber shoots the breeze with team owner Dietrich Mateschitz.

MARK WEBBER

Mark is accustomed to putting one over his team-mates. This year, he has Formula One's hottest new hot shot, Sebastian Vettel, for company and fireworks are assured. But, if the car is good enough, he'll have eyes only for his maiden victory.

Last year, someone called this ultra-competitive Australian "the new Chris Amon." By that, they meant a fabulous driver good enough to win grands prix, but destined never to do so. Let's hope that they're wrong, as Mark is too talented for that, his natural speed, bravery and sheer graft truly deserving of the rewards of the top step of the podium.

On paper, there was an outside chance that last year with Red Bull Racing he would have a chance to try and take on top teams Ferrari and McLaren, with Adrian Newey expected to produce a gem of a chassis. Combining this with a Renault engine was thought to be a better bet than a Ferrari engine, with the Italian power being kept with Dietrich Mateschitz's junior team: Toro Rosso. Whether this was the right way around remains open to debate, but the subservient Toro Rosso changed its spots and it was very hard, in particular, on Mark.

For 2009, he will be joined by Toro Rosso's shining star Sebastian Vettel and it's probably going to be the most interesting

It's almost as though Mark is looking to the other page to size up his new team-mate.

combination out there, the young tyro against the old head. Well, he's 32...

Let's wait and see, but Mark's expertise in the gung-ho lap will stretch and perhaps embarrass Vettel. Or maybe not... But

one thing is clear, and this is that Mark deserves a change of fortune. All too often over the years his best drives have ended in mechanical failure, although there was a great step in the right direction on that front in 2008. Just once, though, it would be right to see him on the podium again in the season ahead.

TRACK NOTES

Nationality:	AUSTRALIAN
Born:	27 AUGUST, 1976, QUEANBEYAN, AUSTRALIA
Website:	www.markwebber.com
Teams:	MINARDI 2002, JAGUAR 2003-2004, WILLIAMS 2005-2006, RED BULL RACING 2007-2009

CAREER RECORD	
First Grand Prix:	2002 AUSTRALIAN GP
Grand Prix starts:	122
Grand Prix wins:	0
	best result: third, 2005 Monaco GP, 2007 European GP
Poles:	0
Fastest laps:	0
	Points: 100
Honours:	2001 FORMULA 3000 RUNNER-UP, 1998 FIA GT RUNNER-UP, 1996 BRITISH FORMULA FORD RUNNER-UP & FORMULA FORD FESTIVAL WINNER

HELPED BY A RUGBY GREAT

Mark has had to work for what he has achieved. This son of a motorcycle dealer hustled his way through Formula Ford in Australia, made it to Britain and his win in the Formula Ford Festival in 1996 was key to securing finance for his graduation to Formula Three, with rugby ace David Campese helping to find the money. A win ought to have helped him on to Formula 3000, but a lack of cash meant that he had to accept Mercedes' invitation to race sports cars. He made it to Formula 3000 in 2000 and was second to Justin Wilson in 2001, by which time he had tested for Benetton and Flavio Briatore helped him land a Formula One ride with Minardi. Fifth first time out was a fluke, but Mark showed his speed for Jaguar before joining Williams. This ought to have been a dream relationship, but wasn't and he has enjoyed life much more since joining Red Bull Racing in 2007.

SEBASTIAN VETTEL

The next few years have the potential to be classic ones as there's a host of truly brilliant newcomers. Think Lewis Hamilton, think Robert Kubica and most definitely think Sebastian Vettel, a driver who looks fresh-faced but has a very wise head.

From the moment Sebastian started racing for Toro Rosso, the crew loved him. He was personable, he was hard working and he was quick. Four retirements and a 17th place finish weren't much of a return from the first five races, but he romped home fifth when let loose in the 2008 car in round six, at Monaco. For a team that has spent most of its life at the back of the field, when it raced as Minardi, it celebrated extra hard for every point earned.

Sebastian then got ever better, exciting the German fans enough for newspaper headlines to refer to him as "the new Michael Schumacher." This he didn't like: he wanted to be the first Sebastian Vettel, very much his own man.

Described as something of a "rough diamond" by Toro Rosso technical director Giorgio Ascanelli, Sebastian could certainly deliver in qualifying and never was this more important than for the Italian GP when conditions were wet. Starting from pole was made an even greater advantage

Don't be fooled by the baby-faced smile, this driver is definitely no easy touch.

when the race was started behind a safety car, meaning that he couldn't be passed, but Sebastian simply didn't put a wheel wrong all race and demonstrated calmness

in extreme conditions, even having the audacity to attack to increase his lead on the way to his first win. It was just the sort of story that Formula One needed.

Promoted to Red Bull Racing for 2009, Sebastian will have to hope that the Renault engines behind his shoulders are as good as the Ferrari V8 he had last year. One thing that is for certain is that he will find Mark Webber a harder team-mate to break.

TRACK NOTES

Nationality:	GERMAN
Born:	3 JULY, 1987, HEEPENHEIM, GERMANY
Website:	www.sebastianvettel.de
Teams:	BMW SAUBER 2007,
	TORO ROSSO 2007-08, RED BULL RACING 2009

CAREER RECORD

First Grand Prix:	2007 UNITED STATES GP
Grand Prix starts:	35
Grand Prix wins:	1
	2008 Italian GP
Poles:	1
Fastest laps:	0
Points:	41
Honours:	2006 EUROPEAN FORMULA 3
	RUNNER-UP, 2004 GERMAN FORMULA BMW
	CHAMPION, 2003 GERMAN FORMULA BMW
	RUNNER-UP, 2001 EUROPEAN & GERMAN
	JUNIOR KART CHAMPION

GERMANY'S NEW GLORY BOY

Some drivers make it to Formula One with only a handful of victories under their belts, having graduated with good results rather than championship titles. Sebastian is not one of these. National and European champion in karting, he made an instant impact when he graduated to car racing in 2003 as a 16-year-old. Racing in Formula BMW, he won five races and then thrashed the opposition in 2004, winning 18 of the 20 races. He was then the top rookie in European Formula Three in 2005. BMW duly gave Sebastian a Formula One test drive. Staying on for a second year, he won four times to be runner-up, but his highlight was becoming BMW Sauber's third driver, at just 19, after Jacques Villenueve left. He then combined his third driver role with racing in the World Series by Renault in 2007, winning the second race, but quit after his impressive race debut in the US GP led to him replacing Scott Speed at Toro Rosso.

WILLIAMS

Things can only get better for this once great team as it was way too erratic to stay at the front of the midfield battle last year. Team founders Williams and Head won't accept another year in which points are a rarity rather than the norm.

Nico Rosberg will be anxious to be in the points more often in 2009.

It's not true to say that there is no change at Williams for the 2009 World Championship. Certainly, the team structure remains just the same, with Sam Michael leading the technical direction. The drivers are the same too, as Nico Rosberg stays for a fourth season and Kazuki Nakajima for a second. The top management is as rock solid as ever, with Sir Frank Williams maintaining an overview and Patrick Head keeping an eye on the machinery as they have for more than 600 grands prix. The engines will be the same, too, coming from Toyota.

So, what changes? The cars, with this year's comprehensive technical revamping being the team's only real hope of making its way up the order, back up to the lofty heights that it enjoyed for so long in the 1980s and first half of the 1990s.

It's a major new roll of the dice and, to be frank, it's the team's only hope of being able to take a crack at the teams with which it used to rub shoulders on the podium, namely Ferrari and McLaren. This is the chance for teams that aren't financially overendowed, like Williams, to take on the big rollers again. It's an opportunity for them to find the sweet spot of the new-shape front and rear wings in particular. Indeed, Williams was the first team to try them out in testing early last autumn.

That there should be so much angst about what lies ahead for Williams seems extraordinary after Rosberg started last year on the podium at the Australian GP, delighted with his third place result. The fact that he and rookie team-mate Nakajima finished no higher than seventh in the next 13 grands prix sadly reflected the true picture.

However, Williams are nothing if not dogged and their car was marginally more competitive as the season advanced before tailing off again in the closing grands prix, although Rosberg's second place, including a drivethrough penalty in Singapore, owed more than a little to the deployment of the safety car at precisely the right moment.

One factor that is a major concern for Williams is the spectre of customer cars, as this has meant that teams junior to it, such as Scuderia Toro Rosso, have been able to buy chassis developed by the leading, well-funded teams and vault past them. This is why this year's rules revolution is so important to Williams.

One of the Williams team's considerations over the winter will have been to ensure that their FW31 gets heat into tyres for qualifying, as last year's car's relatively rearward weight distribution was deficient in this, putting the drivers behind cars that were slower than them in race trim and thus held them up, keeping them from points.

The other shortfall that the design team will have focused on for the new car is making sure that it can cope with high-speed corners, as that was a definite weakness last year.

The reliability was rock-solid last year, but you can be sure that the drivers would trade that solidity for a greater helping of speed, even if that was allied to the odd mechanical failure.

There were natural concerns before last year that Williams might embarrass its engine supplier Toyota by out performing it. The disaparity in their budgets meant that this didn't happen, yet you can't help but feel that after such a weak 2008 they wouldn't mind trying.

FOR THE RECORD

Country of origin:	England
Team base:	Grove, England
Telephone:	(44) 01235 777700
Website:	www.attwilliams.com
Active in Formula One:	From 1972
Grands Prix contested:	568
Wins:	113
Pole positions:	125
Fastest laps:	129

2008 DRIVERS & RESULTS

Driver	Nationality	Races	Wins	Pts	Pos
Kazuki Nakajima	Japanese	18	-	9	15th
Nico Rosberg	German	18	-	17	13th

THE TEAM

Team principal:	Sir Frank Williams
Director of engineering:	Patrick Head
Chief executive officer:	Adam Parr
Technical director:	Sam Michael
Chief operating officer:	Alex Burns
Chief designer:	Ed Wood
Head of aerodynamics:	Jon Tomlinson
Senior systems engineer:	John Russell
Chief operations engineer:	Rod Nelson
Team manager:	Tim Newton
Test drivers:	Nico Hulkenberg
Chassis:	Williams FW31
Engine:	Toyota V8
Tyres:	Bridgestone

Sir Frank Williams doesn't have a top budget, but continues to push.

NICO ROSBERG

As autumn turned to winter last year, Nico commented that his star was seen to be waning, and this must have been particularly galling for a driver who'd just had his best ever season masked by driving a Williams that couldn't compete at the front.

This year, his fourth in Formula One, Nico knows that he must deliver and will have spent the close-season praying that he is blessed with the machinery with which to do the job, as last year he was caught short. He knows that momentum is everything in Formula One and last year's hotshot is soon forgotten if another comes along at the wheel of a more competitive car.

Don't forget that Nico stunned everyone on his Formula One debut in the opening race of 2006 by setting the race's fastest lap. He's set none since.

To this end, last year was cruel for it began with a false dawn, and Nico can't be blamed for having started to believe that this could be the year. Yet, it wasn't to be, as the Toyota-powered Williams FW30 certainly didn't develop into Formula One's weapon of choice.

It started well enough, with Nico finishing third at the opening round in Australia to join his karting team-mate

Nico loved his two podium visits last year but needs a better car to show off his skills.

Lewis Hamilton on the podium, but 14th place at the following round brought him back to earth with a jolt and the year had precious few highlights thereafter. Yes, there was the surprise second place in Singapore, but that owed more than a little to the timing of the deployment of the safety car.

Having a World Champion for a father would be difficult for any young racer. Just ask Nelson Piquet Jr. But, one feels that the task is even harder for Nico as his father Keke left such a large shadow, being a swashbuckling individual with an on-the-edge style. Nico is cut from a very different cloth, being far more urbane, but he may yet have his day.

TRACK NOTES

Nationality:	GERMAN
Born:	27 JUNE, 1985, WIESBADEN, GERMANY
Website:	www.nicorosberg.com
Teams:	WILLIAMS 2006-2009

CAREER RECORD

First Grand Prix:	2006 BAHRAIN GP
Grand Prix starts:	53
Grand Prix wins:	0
best result: second, 2008 Singapore GP	
Poles:	0
Fastest laps:	1
Points:	41
Honours:	2005 GP2 CHAMPION, 2002
	FORMULA BMW CHAMPION

SON OF HIS FATHER

Urged on by his father, Keke, young Nico raced karts through his youth, often in the same team as a young Lewis Hamilton. He was, perhaps inevitably, the less successful of this duo, but Nico's results were far from shabby as he also continued his schooling to a high level at the same time. When they reached car racing in the same year, 2002, Nico made his father smile by doing something that Lewis failed to do: he became a champion at his first attempt, winning the German Formula BMW crown. Whereas Keke raced in numerous formulae, anywhere on the globe, to keep his career in the ascendancy, turning out almost every weekend from spring to winter, Nico was able to concentrate on European Formula Three, ranking fourth in 2004, before winning the GP2 title at his first attempt the following year, just ahead of Heikki Kovalainen. And so, fittingly, he reached Formula One in 2006 with the team with which his father scored his title win: Williams.

KAZUKI NAKAJIMA

Team-mate Nico Rosberg was the glory boy, the focus of attention when people considered Williams, but Kazuki's efforts deserved not to be overlooked as he showed the sort of grit when the going got tough that this team of fighters love.

As with all reviews of the Williams team's 2008 campaign, it has to be taken into account that what had started well in pre-season testing unravelled increasingly as the year advanced. Perhaps this explains how Kazuki started the season with sixth place in Australia - his second grand prix start - although his was actually last of the seven cars still running. It explains too how he scored three of his four other points drives by mid-season and collected just one eighth place thereafter, in Singapore.

To do your learning in a car that was up and down, but sadly increasingly down, in terms of form must have been dispiriting, but the team marvelled at how Kazuki seemed to thrive in adversity, managing to bring his car home in races in which the going had been tough when drivers of greater experience and superior talents didn't. So, he had application rather than just raw speed and reversed opinion of him that he was simply fast and furious, something that had been compounded when he bowled

Kazuki displayed an incredible ability to score points in the toughest races last year.

over his pit crew on his Formula One debut in the 2007 Brazilian GP.

For any son of a former grand prix driver, one's arrival in Formula One is always

regarded with suspicion, people saying it was family name rather than talent that clinched the deal. In Kazuki's case, this suspicion was made worse as he was said to have been given his promotion from GP2 solely because he came as part of a package with Toyota engines that Williams use. This may have been the case, and it probably was, but there is an increasing feeling that Kazuki might yet be able to hold his own on the sport's biggest stage. Providing Williams can get it right with the new car rules, we will find out this year.

TRACK NOTES

Nationality:	JAPANESE
Born:	11 JANUARY, 1985, AICHI, JAPAN
Website:	www.kazuki-nakajima.com
Teams:	WILLIAMS 2007-2009

CAREER RECORD	
First Grand Prix:	2007 BRAZILIAN GP
Grand Prix starts:	19
Grand Prix wins:	0
	best result: sixth, 2008 Australian GP
Poles:	0
Fastest laps:	0
Points:	9
Honours:	2005 JAPANESE FORMULA THREE RUNNER-UP, 2003 JAPANESE FORMULA TOYOTA CHAMPION

NOT JUST FAST AND FURIOUS

To have three sons of former grand prix drivers among Formula One's current crop of 20 drivers is extraordinary, but Kazuki has the fewest bragging rights as his is the odd one out, never a winner on the sport's biggest stage. As with all of his rivals, Kazuki spent his teenage years racing karts before stepping up to Formula Toyota in Japan, winning the title at his first attempt in 2003. That encouraged Toyota to sign him for its crack Formula Three team, which must have felt strange for his father Satoru who was a longtime Honda man, and he finished as runner-up in 2005. He learned the circuits in European Formula Three in 2006 then moved up to GP2 and showed flashes of blinding speed, but an erratic streak too, with a second place his best. However, a late-season outing for Williams helped him hit Formula One and prove that he could perform to the required level, without any help from his famous father.

TEAM X (PREVIOUSLY HONDA RACING)

This team was Formula One's worst underachiever last year, but it came as a thunderbolt when Honda closed it in December. Buyers were sought, at a knockdown price, but its participation remained a serious doubt.

Jenson Button can only be hoping that he'll race in 2009

Whichever of the dozen potential takeover bids succeeds, and there were a dozen when this book closed for press, there will be a mountain to climb to make up for the disruption over the winter

Two bad years in succession knocked the stuffing out of Honda's Formula One team, and last year's world championship was painful to watch as two drivers of merit, grand prix winners both, struggled to keep anyone other than Force India behind them. Even keeping the Toro Rossos in sight would have been an achievement, and these were cars that everyone expected them to beat, easily.

Certainly, the difference between success and failure has never been so small in Formula One's midfield. One slip in qualifying, losing just tenths of a second, can wreck an entire grand prix meeting, make points out of reach rather than a formality. And so it was that Rubens Barrichello and Jenson Button struggled through 2008.

Perhaps Barrichello summed it up best when he said, honestly, about his hopes of retaining his ride for 2009: "It's almost like you deserve the seat because the car has been so bad for the past two years..."

For the sake of the drivers, at least the team management, from technical director Ross Brawn down, understood their plight, knew that they were robbing Peter to pay Paul by

TEAM VIPS

ROSS BRAWN
Big Ross has been there and done that, getting into the sport via a spell as a machinist at Williams. He became the team's chief aerodynamicist by 1979 and held a similar post at Force before becoming Arrows' chief designer in 1986. Success in sports cars followed when TWR ran the Jaguar team, then it was back to Formula One with Benetton, winning titles with Michael Schumacher before repeating the feat, and more, with Michael at Ferrari prior to joining Honda for 2008.

NICK FRY
One of the few involved in Formula One to have reached the sport via the motor industry, Nick joined Ford in 1978 and had a spell as managing director of Aston Martin in the 1990s before joining the Prodrive motorsport engineering concern in 2001. He then landed in Formula One in 2002 to support its chief David Richards who was also heading up BAR. Richards left in 2004 and Fry stayed on in charge, staying on as Honda took over.

investing in 2009 rather than doing development work on the 2008 car from the end of July onwards. And, in contemporary Formula One, to stand still is to go backwards, which is what happened to Barrichello and Button. They simply had to grin and bear it, and pray that 2009 would be worth it.

Glance at the last year's results and a well-earned weather-induced third place finish for Barrichello in the British GP was by far the team's highlight.

After the full winter of testing it had planned, the team ought to have been in better shape than ever before, but then came the snag: the parent company pulled the plug. All that promise was going to be latent. Unless a buyer could be found, and fast...

Perhaps the sudden need to find a buyer was a direct result of Brawn having sacrificed 2008 for 2009, in reckoning that the wholesale changes in the technical regulations offered the team the best chance to shuffle the established order, to put one over the likes of Ferrari and McLaren. It was an all-or-nothing gamble, but no-one could have foreseen the consequences would be so dire. Well, the consequences aided and abetted by the global economic downturn. To say that the shockwaves Honda's withdrawal triggered were massive was an understatement and talk was immediately that other teams must also fold.

However, all potential buyers were encouraged that Honda would probably sweeten the deal

as much as possible. Former team boss David Richards was among the early bidders, but pulled out of the running, by which time there were said to be a dozen serious parties, with a management buy-out becoming the most likely as we closed for press, with the possibility of Brawn's involvement

attracting Michael Schumacher to become an investor.

What they would purchase is a fabulous facility in Brackley and some top-rate personnel, but with Formula One keen to cut its cloth according to more sensible outlines, it would have to be run as a much tighter ship.

FOR THE RECORD

Country of origin:	England
Team base:	Brackley, England
Telephone:	(44) 01280 844000
Website:	www.hondaracingf1.com
Active in Formula One:	From 1999 (as BAR)
Grands Prix contested:	171
Wins:	1
Pole positions:	3
Fastest laps:	0

2008 DRIVERS & RESULTS

Driver	Nationality	Races	Wins	Pts	Pos
Rubens Barrichello	Brazilian	18	-	11	14th
Jenson Button	British	18	-	3	18th

THE TEAM

Chairman:	tba
Team principal:	Ross Brawn
Chief executive officer:	Nick Fry
Technical director:	Jorg Zander
Engineering director:	Jacky Eeckelaert
Operations director:	Gary Savage
Chief designer:	Kevin Taylor
Head of aerodynamics:	Loic Bigois
Chief engineer:	Craig Wilson
Sporting director:	Ron Meadows
Test driver:	tba
Chassis:	tba
Engine:	tba
Tyres:	Bridgestone

Ross Brawn took a gamble on 2009 and may never find out if it worked.

JENSON BUTTON

It's nine years since Jenson was the fresh-faced ace who vaulted into Formula One. Experience was added to speed that year and race wins would surely follow. One did, in 2006, but he's yet to race for a top team and now perhaps never will.

The role of a driver is to get into anything with four wheels and drive it faster than anyone else. The role of a driver manager is to make sure that his charge is in the most competitive machinery. Somehow, despite all Jenson's latent ability, the ducks have never been lined up in a row and neither Ferrari nor McLaren have signed him up.

When conditions become treacherous and changeable, Jenson is your man, as proved when he won in Hungary. This was for Honda, and the fact that he had to progress from 14th on the grid said it all.

Yet, through 2008, as Honda lost more ground as all energies were focused on their 2009 challenger, you had to look hard to find Jenson. His biggest chance was in the wet-dry British GP, but he slid off the circuit. The rewards were there to be taken that day, as shown by team-mate Rubens Barrichello coming home third. That Jenson scored just three points all year made this slip-up all the more galling.

Jenson can't wait to get his hands on a car with which to shoot for his second victory.

On other occasions, the team sent Jenson out on increasingly unusual race strategies in the hope of helping him up the order past faster cars. You couldn't help but feel that his was a talent going to waste.

There were times in the closing races when Barrichello became more competitive that people feared for Jenson keeping his ride, but he held on and must hope that Ross Brawn and Geoff Willis have crafted a car that will get him into the points if he is to have a chance of taking his second win..

TRACK NOTES

Nationality:	BRITISH
Born:	19 JANUARY, 1980, FROME, ENGLAND
Website:	www.jensonbutton.com
Teams:	WILLIAMS 2000, BENETTON/RENAULT 2001-2002, BAR/HONDA 2003-2009

CAREER RECORD

First Grand Prix:	2000 AUSTRALIAN GP
Grand Prix starts:	154
Grand Prix wins:	1
	2006 Hungarian GP
Poles:	3
Fastest laps:	0
Points:	232
Honours:	1999 MACAU FORMULA THREE RUNNER-UP, 1998 FORMULA FORD FESTIVAL WINNER, BRITISH FORMULA FORD CHAMPION & McLAREN AUTOSPORT BRDC YOUNG DRIVER, 1997 EUROPEAN SUPER A KART CHAMPION, 1991 BRITISH CADET KART CHAMPION

PROMISE AND FRUSTRATION

Before Lewis Hamilton came along, there was another star who won everything in karting then made a huge impact on car racing. It was Jenson, and he won the British Formula Ford title at his first attempt. He moved up to Formula Three for 1999, even starting his first race from pole, but had to settle for third overall, which was still sensational for a rookie, especially one with so little car racing experience. While pondering whether to do a second year of Formula Three or move up to Formula 3000, Jenson tested for Prost and went so well that he found himself in a shoot-out for the second Williams ride for 2000. He got it and seemed unable to do any wrong, going faster with every race. Moving to Benetton for 2001 was when the frustration set in, though, as he was faced with an uncompetitive car for the first time and the pain only eased when he moved team and BAR came good in 2004 and he ranked third overall. Apart from his victory for Honda in Hungary in 2006, the frustration has continued.

BRUNO SENNA

The incredibly strong desire for having racing dynasties in Formula One has struck again and the late great Ayrton Senna's nephew Bruno has been picked by Honda, and now it's up to him to show that he has talent to match.

Honda was increasingly excited last year about the possibility of signing Bruno to fill its second seat to run as junior driver to Jenson Button in 2009. You might ask that if Honda was so interested in having a Brazilian driver so it could have a foothold in this important South American automotive market, why didn't it keep multiple grand prix winner Rubens Barrichello. But this is to fail to understand the link between Honda and Senna. Not so much Bruno yet, but Ayrton who was all but worshipped in Japan when he won races in a Honda-powered Lotus in 1987 then raced to three world titles with a Honda engine in his McLaren, taking time out to help develop its exquisite NSX sports car, a car with supreme handling.

Bruno is different, especially as he has considerably less racing experience than the majority of his rivals, having not done kart racing, but he's a bright boy and a quick learner, listening to advice tendered to help make up for lost time. This was clear as he knuckled down first to Formula Three

His uncle is a tough act to follow but Bruno Senna has proved a determined character.

then GP2. A good budget can take you only so far and no mug wins at GP2 level.

And now, thank you, Bruno says he's ready for Formula One. Which is where Honda comes in...

The helmet design is the same as his late uncle's – yellow with a blue stripe and a green stripe – but the unbelievable speed that Ayrton could conjure has yet to be seen. On the evidence of Bruno's career so far, though, you feel that he's working on it. And, like all second generation racers, he'd love to be considered on his own merits rather than someone else's.

TRACK NOTES

Nationality:	BRAZILIAN
Born:	15 APRIL, 1982, SAO PAULO, BRAZIL
Website:	www.brunosenna.co.br
Teams:	HONDA 2009

CAREER RECORD

First Grand Prix:	2009 AUSTRALIAN GP
Grand Prix starts:	0
Grand Prix wins:	0
Poles:	0
Fastest laps:	0
Points:	0
Honours:	2008 GP2 RUNNER-UP

LEARNING AS HE GOES

Bruno experienced what it was like to drive a kart when he was little. But his uncle Ayrton's death when Bruno was 12 meant that his family didn't want him to race one. However, his mother Viviane relented when Bruno said he wanted to go car racing. He was 22 by then and contested a few rounds of the British Formula BMW series in 2004 racing, of course, against people who had competed for years. Bruno had to learn as he went along, doing so in British Formula Three in 2005 and twice finishing second as he ranked 10th. Back for more in 2006, he won the first three rounds, going on to end the year an impressive third overall. Winning on only his third outing in GP2 in 2007 marked Bruno out, but there were no more wins. However, Bruno bounced back last year with iSport International, winning twice before a run of poor results left him as runner-up Giorgio to Pantano.

FORCE INDIA F1

Vijay Mallya isn't a man who does anything by half-measures, as shown by his decision to sign a five-year technical partnership with McLaren-Mercedes to supply Force India with engines, drivetrain and KERS systems. This is a man who means business.

Giancarlo Fisichella is excited by the team's deal for Mercedes engines.

Last year was a struggle for Force India. Billionaire team owner Vijay Mallya didn't expect anything else, as he hadn't come on board early enough for his money to influence the car's design. In fact, finances had been so tight that the VJM01 was merely an update of the 2007 car. At least introducing a seamless-shift gearbox helped mid-season, finding the drivers as much as 0.3-0.4s per lap when it was introduced for the Hungarian GP, but this year there will be an all-new car and so no excuses will be allowed and championship points will be expected.

The deal for the change of engine for this year's World Championship was negotiated just as last year's action came to a close, and it is expected that there will be a transfer of technology from McLaren as well as the use of Mercedes V8s in place of the Ferrari engines that Force India used last year, with McLaren gearboxes and KERS as part of the deal.

If this doesn't take the team forward, nothing will.

It's safe to say that there was trouble in the air at Force India last year and you can draw your own conclusions as to the direction of the lively debate by the fact that team principal Colin Kolles and chief technical officer Mike Gascoyne weren't invited to stay on when the

PAST LEGENDS

VIJAY MALLYA
A racer in his own right in his younger days, flamboyant Vijay is better known as a businessman, leading India's UB Group, a multi-product group of companies that ranks Kingfisher beer as one of its most famous brands and Vijay married this to Formula One with Benetton in 1996. He liked what he saw, went away and made even more money. Identifying that India is one of Formula One's growth areas, he wisely bought the failing Spyker (once Jordan) team and renamed it Force India F1 for 2008.

MARK SMITH
Force India's design director took a mechanical engineering degree and moved into motorsport with a branch of the March group in 1988. A move to Reynard in 1989 led to him working on its F3000 design before he started a 10-year stint as design director at Jordan. He transferred to Renault as chief designer in 2001, but moved on to Red Bull Racing as technical director in 2005 before returning to this team that was once Jordan.

deal was done with McLaren-Mercedes. Commercial director Patrick Missling also left.

Coming in to take the helm of the day-to-day running of the team is Simon Roberts, fittingly from McLaren, to be chief operating officer.

Gascoyne had spent much of last year realigning the technical side of the team while Mark Smith was overseeing the car, working with ex-Toyota staffman Ian Hall on the 2009 car, with James Key taking a technical overview. So, perhaps the change won't be so great. And focus on this car they most certainly did, as they gave up on last year's car as early as July.

While there were too many mechanical failures in 2008 and the team is extra keen to eliminate these, the drivers also had to hold their hands up for more than the odd accident.

Continuity can be extremely important in motor racing and it's even more so for a team that is trying to make strides up the ranking, so Mallya was quick to announce last autumn that he was re-signing his drivers, the hugely experienced Giancarlo Fisichella and the fast but inconsistent Adrian Sutil.

Neither scored a point last year, although no one will forget what happened to Sutil at Monaco, when he was punted out of fourth place by Kimi Raikkonen's out-of-control Ferrari. The loss was more than just galling, as it meant that Force India failed to score all year, costing the team millions in prize money. Monaco aside, the team's best result all campaign was Fisichella's 10th place in the Spanish GP.

The only other real highlight of last season for Force India was when a decision to be the first on to dry weather tyres in the early laps of the Brazilian GP led to Fisichella vaulting up the order from 19th to actually lead for a few laps. And you can be sure that Mallya didn't mind at all when Fisichella's car filled TV screens the world over as he held off Lewis Hamilton's McLaren for a few laps, often pulling clear out of the corners.

Expectations for 2009 are rather higher, though.

Vijay Mallya expects results and he's shown his ruthless side already.

FOR THE RECORD

Country of origin:	England
Team base:	Silverstone, England
Telephone:	(44) 01327 850800
Website:	www.forceindia.com
Active in Formula One:	From 1991 (as Jordan then Midland in 2006 then Spyker in 2007)
Grands Prix contested:	303
Wins:	4
Pole positions:	2
Fastest laps:	2

2008 DRIVERS & RESULTS

Driver	Nationality	Races	Wins	Pts	Pos
Giancarlo Fisichella	Italian	18	0	0	n/a
Adrian Sutil	German	18	0	0	n/a

THE TEAM

Team owner:	Vijay Mallya
Co-owner:	Michiel Mol
Chief operating officer:	Simon Roberts
Technical director:	James Key
Design director:	Mark Smith
Head of R&D:	Simon Garner
Head of aerodynamics:	Simon Phillips
Team manager:	Andy Stevenson
Chief engineer:	Dominic Harlow
Test driver:	tba
Chassis:	VJM02
Engine:	Mercedes V8
Tyres:	Bridgestone

GIANCARLO FISICHELLA

It was said last year that Giancarlo was drinking at Formula One's last chance saloon. Well, he must have enjoyed it, as he's back for more, bringing the experience of one of the grand prix scene's elder statesmen to help guide the team forward.

Money is seen as the prime motivator for some drivers, ranked above any sporting aspirations, but Giancarlo has never been seen as such a man. He's not in it for the yachts, the private islands and other trappings. No, he's a racer, pure and simple. However, with his own team operating in the junior formulae and a family at home, you have to wonder when he will want to call it quits. After all, it's not as though he has an outside chance of victory with Force India. It would have taken a gale force following wind to blow him as far forward as the midfield last year, and that's no place for a three-time grand prix winner.

Still, Force India team owner Vijay Mallya wants him on board for the experience that Giancarlo has gained over his 13 years in Formula One, during which time he has four years under his belt with this team that was once Jordan.

Looking to 2009, with the rule changes and the full force of Mallya's billions being felt for the first time, does Giancarlo have

Giancarlo will be praying that a superior car will help him to rise from the tail of the field.

a hope of adding a fourth win to his tally? No, clearly, but he might be able to score a point or two, and that's all it can ask as it strives to advance towards the midfield.

Paired for a second year with the fast but inconsistent Adrian Sutil, he will want at least to put the youngster in the shade. Indeed, with a tally of 267 career points to one, you'd expect him to. Yet, at this stage in his career, there remains the question over whether Giancarlo is prepared to take that ultimate risk anymore.

This year will provide the answer.

TRACK NOTES

Nationality:	ITALIAN
Born:	14 JANUARY, 1973, ROME, ITALY
Website:	www.giancarlofisichella.it
Teams:	MINARDI 1996, JORDAN 1997 &
	2002-2003, BENETTON 1998-2001, SAUBER 2004,
	RENAULT 2005-2007, FORCE INDIA 2008-2009

CAREER RECORD	
First Grand Prix:	1996 AUSTRALIAN GP
Grand Prix starts:	214
Grand Prix wins:	3
	2003 Brazilian GP, 2005
	Australian GP, 2006 Malaysian GP
Poles:	3
Fastest laps:	2
Points:	267
Honours:	1994 ITALIAN FORMULA THREE
	CHAMPION & MONACO FORMULA
	THREE WINNER, 1991 EUROPEAN KART
	RUNNER-UP, 1990 WORLD KART RUNNER-UP,

ITALY'S KARTING HOTSHOT

Giancarlo must have one of the largest collections of kart trophies anywhere, as he spent his childhood collecting them around Italy. It was only when he ventured beyond Italy's borders that he found people who could beat him. Second overall in the European series in 1991 was enough to pitch him into Formula Runner-up in 1993, he was Italian champion in 1994, also winning the race supporting the Monaco GP. But then came the hitch; Giancarlo didn't have enough money to move on to Formula 3000. So Alfa Romeo snapped him up to race one of its cars in the International Touring Car Championship and he did well. Then Minardi grabbed him back for 1996 and he has been in Formula One ever since, enjoying strong form for Jordan in 1997 and then for Benetton. A second spell at Jordan brought a weird win in Brazil in 2003 and Giancarlo added two more for Renault before joining Force India for his swansong.

ADRIAN SUTIL

In a full season, it's incredible that fans will remember Adrian's second year in Formula One for just one drive. For Monaco, where he was heading for an incredible fourth until being punted out by Kimi Raikkonen. He'd rather score points in 2009.

Yes, that was a Force India being taken out of a race by a Ferrari that was running, on merit, behind it. It was amazing and remains one of the saddest sights of 2008, as the white, gold and red car was shunted into the chicane by the Finn's Ferrari in the closing laps, costing fourth place, five points and considerable acclaim.

In so many ways, this sums up Adrian's career. It suggests speed, which he has. It suggests a lack of meaningful results, which is also true. But, then again, when you're driving for a tail-end team, what else would you expect?

When you looked to Adrian and team-mate Giancarlo Fisichella last year, you always expected the fireworks to come from the youngster. Indeed, they did. There were flashes of brilliance, but seldom when it counted, usually coming in a wet practice session. It counted for nought, but it still logged in the minds of the team chiefs and the journalists in the media centre. I'm sure that team boss Vijay Mallya also

Adrian finished fewer than half of last year's races and must improve on that this year.

wasn't averse to seeing his car on camera.

For 2009, though, Adrian is no longer a novice. Certainly, the many opening lap errors of his rookie season in 2007 are now a thing of the past, long behind him, but there were still more retirements than finishes last year and that must change if he is ever to line himself up a transfer to a team at the sharp end of the grid.

Adrian will want all of the attention in 2009 to be positive, unlike one incident last year when a German citizen got hold of a hard drive out of his old computer and tried to blackmail him with it, in return for a cash pay-out that he never got.

TRACK NOTES

Nationality: GERMAN

Born: 11 JANUARY 1983, GRAFELFING, GERMANY

Website: www.adriansutil.com

Teams: SPYKER/FORCE INDIA 2007-2009

CAREER RECORD

First Grand Prix: 2007 AUSTRALIAN GP

Grand Prix starts: 35

Grand Prix wins: 0

best result: eighth, 2007 Japanese GP

Poles: 0

Fastest laps: 0

Points: 1

Honours: 2006 JAPANESE FORMULA THREE CHAMPION, 2005 EUROPEAN FORMULA THREE RUNNER-UP, 2002 SWISS FORMULA FORD CHAMPION

HITTING ALL THE RIGHT NOTES

Had Adrian followed his father's career path, he would have been a classical musician. As it was, he was hooked by karting and did well enough for the family to invest in his move into cars. Although a champion in Formula Ford, albeit in the minor Swiss series, what is clear is the way that he improved with every further year, even giving team-mate Lewis Hamilton a run for his money when they raced in the European Formula Three series in 2005. Ending the year as runner-up to Hamilton, Adrian advanced to race Germany's car in A1GP in before former Formula Three boss Colin Kolles invited him to be Spyker's third driver at the end of 2006. He did well enough and became a fully-fledged Formula One racer the following year, albeit showing a propensity to end his races on the opening lap before calming down and producing a stunning performance in practice at the Monaco GP, when he lapped fastest of all in the wet.

TALKING POINT: **TECHNICAL CHANGES FOR 2009**

Continuity is important to designers and engineers, but technical changes for this year will have kept them on their toes. The reversion to slick tyres is the most obvious, but it's the wholesale reduction of aerodynamics that will have vexed them the most.

The most obvious technical change is the return of slick tyres, bringing an end to an 11-year run for grooved tyres. At a stroke, memories of earlier decades will be triggered, such as the battles between James Hunt and Niki Lauda in 1976, or Nigel Mansell versus Williams team-mate Nelson Piquet in 1986, or even the great inter-McLaren fights between Ayrton Senna and Alain Prost a few years later all on big, fat, slick tyres.

The key to slicks is that they look fit for purpose, fit for getting as much rubber on to the track as possible to aid with grip for cornering and traction for acceleration, matters made all the more important since traction control was banned in 2008.

Tyre supplier Bridgestone has said that it will also try to add to the show by making the difference between the two tyre compounds it brings to each round more marked so that it's easier for fans to understand who is running on what compound at which point in the grand prix and so to anticipate what that driver might expect from their next set of tyres when they have to change to the alternate compound.

With the difference between compounds being magnified for 2009, the strategy and length of stints is sure to be all the more variable and hopefully will lead to more see-sawing of race order, thus more overtaking.

In a bid to encourage overtaking, the teams have been given a target of cutting downforce by 50% through the reduction in size of bargeboards and diffuser, the removal of flip-ups, winglets, chimneys and louvres from the top of the sidepods, the narrowing of the rear wing and the use of a front wing with a standard centre section profile. One of the most exciting changes, though, is for the front wing setting to be driver-adjustable to help when following another car.

The third rule change is the introduction of KERS (Kinetic Energy Recovery Systems) that stores energy lost in braking into a battery or a spinning flywheel and turns it into motive power as the driver accelerates out of the corner. It has been calculated that as much as an extra 80bhp can be supplied for a maximum of 6.7 seconds.

KERS surfaced in 1998, with McLaren, but was outlawed, much to the frustration of technical director Adrian Newey. It's only now that Formula One is looking to boost its green credentials that this decision has been reversed, with its possibilities for road car usage clear for all to see.

Adopting KERS has proved a headache for some teams after a mechanic received an electric shock during early testing and there were a couple of battery fires.

As late as August 2008, some teams were pushing to have its introduction delayed, with Toyota among these ranks, even saying last November that it wouldn't have its KERS ready for the opening race in Melbourne, whereas BMW Sauber, Honda and Williams are its most bullish supporters. KERS won't be mandatory, though, allowing those who are not yet ready to race without it.

Wider front wing, up from 1.4m to 1.8m

Lower front wing, down from 150mm to 75mm

Tyres have been changed from grooved to slick, providing an 18% increase in contact area

Bargeboards have been banned, as these generate around 15% of downforce and affect transverse airflow when following another car

Driver-adjustable front wing to adjust front downforce to assist make overtaking easier

Continuous Variable Transmission (CVT) delivers power to and from flywheel and can go from zero to full power in 50 milliseconds

CVT receives energy from driveline during deceleration

Energy released into driveline for acceleration

KINETIC ENERGY RECOVERY SYSTEM

Energy normally lost during deceleration is stored in either an electrical system – like current hybrid road cars – or a mechanical flywheel system

Total weight of system: 24kg

Maximum energy storage capacity: 400 kilojoules

The flywheel is vacuum-sealed, and its composite cylinder rotates at more than 60,000rpm

The angle of the adjustable rollers determines speed delivered to flywheel, or torque from flywheel to driveline. Curved inner surface of discs allows continuously variable ratio change – up to 6-to-1 within one revolution

Winglets have been banned, along with turning vanes and sidepod exhaust chimneys

A larger gap between the planes of the rear wing helps to leave less turbulent wake

The diffuser is longer and set further back to reduce downforce and turbulence

TALKING POINT:
NIGHT RACING

Racing under floodlights added a new dimension to Formula One last September when the Singapore GP dazzled and excited. The result was a resounding success, and now the pressure is on neighbouring Malaysian GP to follow suit, as other grands prix are sure to in the future.

The formula for Formula One has been, since it's inception to follow the sun around the globe, to race in the host country's spring, summer or autumn. Sure, the races would be hit by rain showers from time to time, but the norm was a grand prix starting with the cars glinting in the sunshine.

Then came 2008 and the Singapore GP: this was different, very different, as it started after night had fallen and the only reflections from the cars as they sat on the grid awaiting the start were from the beams of the floodlights.

Night racing wasn't chosen for Singapore's inaugural race simply to make it stand out, rather so that it would fit in better with the waking hours of the all-important European market, Formula One's key set of television viewers. By starting in the evening, the race start would save European fans from having to rise before day break to watch the race.

That the conditions in tropical Singapore were also improved for the drivers and cars, as the typically soaring temperatures in this equatorial setting had cooled as darkness fell, was a bonus.

For the drivers, darkness was simply another factor, and they relied in advance on their teams establishing the level of light that would be available, whether it would be pooled on the corners or constant the length of the lap, asking for it to be dialled in to the

simulation models created to help them get a feel for the new circuit before heading there.

It's not just a question of the amount of light available either, but also the amount of reflection and glare that drivers face when light is coming from many sources rather than just one: the sun. So, the correct visor choice is crucial for night racing.

Then, of course, the teams have to consider the effects of rain to the light put out by the floodlights and also whether the drivers would be able to spot sitting water that could send them crashing off the circuit in an instant.

In true Formula One style, every possibility was considered before the Singapore GP, but the outcome was a race that provided something new and exciting, offering moody and part-shaded images of Formula One that give it a whole new appeal.

For 2009, Malaysia was intending to join the night racing gang as the first purpose-built racing circuit to floodlight its lap, but the cost of doing so in the current economic downturn has delayed this for now, with the race merely being moved back two hours to a 17:00 start for cooler conditions for the drivers and a 10:00 start time for the European viewers.

Expect South Korea and India, when they join the World Championship in the near future with their all-new circuits, to have floodlights on order for this particular purpose.

It doesn't matter from which angle you look at Singapore's Marina Bay circuit, it looked totallly different to anything ever seen before, simply because the racing was at night, with the floodlights adding a moodiness to the downtown circuit as a whole, but most especially to the pitlane

KNOW THE TRACKS 2009

Last year Valencia and Singapore joined the Formula One circus. This year, with the addition of Abu Dhabi, the expansion continues. The teams don't want to expand beyond 19 grands prix, citing exhaustion of their team personnel, but Bernie Ecclestone's ambitions are to take Formula One to yet more of the globe, so brace yourself for more new venues in the years ahead. The other difference is that the Malaysian GP will follow Singapore's lead and be run after dark.

The Formula One calendar is an ever-changing feast, but not all of the changes are additions to the programme. Abu Dhabi is breaking into the show, kicking off with this year's final race, but for Silverstone, the circuit that hosted the first round of the inaugural World Championship in 1950, the end is nigh, and this will be the last British GP that it hosts for some time.

As has almost always been the case in the past decade, the Australian GP will set the ball rolling in March. New for 2009, though, will be a later starting time of 17:00, introduced to enable

Formula One fans in the prime European market to rise at a more reasonable hour to catch the action. Bernie Ecclestone had wanted an even later start time, after darkness had fallen, but the organisers at Melbourne's Albert Park circuit baulked at the cost of installing floodlights. Indeed, those against the race happening there at all would have gone berserk had any more race-related objects been inserted into their favourite green patch.

The next circuit to change its race's start time is Sepang, with the Malaysian GP being pushed back so that it starts after

dark. The fans in the grandstands will welcome the change, as the soaring temperatures will have started dropping by then.

The Bahrain GP retains its place as the third race, no doubt feeling that it must put on an even better show than thus far as near neighbour Abu Dhabi will be making a big splash in 2009.

Then it's back to Europe for the Spanish GP, with fans everywhere praying that some overtaking will be produced there this time around. Another change of pace follows with the first street race of the year, at Monaco. Then it's across the Atlantic for the Canadian GP, with Lewis Hamilton no doubt breaking out into a sweat at the thought of what happened in the pit lane there last June.

The power plays between the circuits and Formula One Management have dictated that the British GP will make its last visit to Silverstone, so it's worth booking your tickets early for one last taste of its wonderful corners before the race heads to Donington Park for 2010.

Bringing the British GP forward to mid-June shuffles the order, with the French GP – possibly the last one at Magny-Cours – now leading onto the German GP. With its circuit alternation now in full swing, it's the Nurburgring's turn in 2009. Next up is the Hungarian GP, but another new feature for 2009 is the loss of the recently-established summer break.

This has led to consternation among the teams and McLaren has taken steps to ensure that its staff won't be burned out by the lack of a chance for a holiday with their families by implementing a staff rotation policy. Others will follow.

The Turkish GP has been moved back to the heat of summer and it's sure to be hot too for Formula One's second visit to Valencia.

With the ever-changing face of Formula One including yet more new supercircuits, the next two races add a welcome dose of the traditional, with the Italian GP at Monza followed a week later by the Belgian GP at the magnificent Spa-Francorchamps. Then it's back to the brave new world of Singapore's night race before the teams continue their journey east for the back-to-back grands prix at Suzuka and Shanghai in Japan and China respectively.

For years, the finale was in Australia but recently it has been in Brazil. Interlagos is next up, but South America's only grand prix won't bring the curtain down on the 2009 season as that honour has been awarded to the year's only new race: the Abu Dhabi GP on 1 November. As the third new street circuit in the past two years, it will add a taste of something very different, which is just what Bernie Ecclestone wants and just where he wants it.

The potential for further expansion is not endless, as the teams aren't keen to go beyond 20 grands prix per year, but expect India to have a race of its own from 2010.

MELBOURNE

There's been considerable debate about the future of the Australian GP in Melbourne's Albert Park, but it has been secured by agreeing to start a little later in the day.

After much wrangling to run the event into a night race so as to suit Formula One fans in Europe, a deal has been done to keep the Australian GP in Melbourne until 2015. The deal was done with a compromise, though, and the one struck was that the race will now start not after dark as had been hoped for, as the installation of floodlights would be too expensive, but at 17:00 instead, which corresponds to 06:00 in the UK rather than the 04:30 start up until now, thus making it more appealing to the television audiences.

Just to keep the race organisers in Melbourne on their toes during the contract negotiations, the Eastern Creek circuit on the outskirts of Sydney started talking of extending its lap and installing lights for a night race, but Melbourne held firm.

Sunny weather is almost always on offer at the Albert Park circuit, making it the perfect place to kick off the season. Better still, the grandstands are always packed and the fans openly enthusiastic.

The first corner isn't tricky in its own right, but trying to funnel 20 cars into there together on the opening lap always provides wheel-banging and often an accident. The entrance to Turn 3, under the trees, is tighter still. On the far side of the lake that the circuit encircles, the track changes its nature and is fast and flowing, but this changes again at Ascari, a tight right-hander. A good exit out of Prost is essential to stand a chance of passing into Turn 1.

INSIDE TRACK

AUSTRALIAN GRAND PRIX

Date:	**29 March**
Circuit name:	**Albert Park**
Circuit length:	**3.295 miles/5.3km**
Number of laps:	**58**
Telephone:	**00 61 3 92587100**
Website:	**www.grandprix.com.au**

PREVIOUS WINNERS

1999	**Eddie Irvine** FERRARI
2000	**Michael Schumacher** FERRARI
2001	**Michael Schumacher** FERRARI
2002	**Michael Schumacher** FERRARI
2003	**David Coulthard** McLAREN
2004	**Michael Schumacher** FERRARI
2005	**Giancarlo Fisichella** RENAULT
2006	**Fernando Alonso** RENAULT
2007	**Kimi Raikkonen** FERRARI
2008	**Lewis Hamilton** McLAREN

Most memorable race: It's hard to pass at Albert Park, so it's no surprise that one of the more memorable moments came when one driver pulled over to let a team-mate by. This was in 1998 when David Coulthard let Mika Hakkinen back into the lead after the Finn had lost the lead when he thought that he'd been called into the pits.

Best for action: Turn 1 is where it happens, almost inevitably on the opening lap. Think back to 2002 when Ralf Schumacher's Williams rocketed off Rubens Barrichello's Ferrari. It's not all accidents at this tight right, as shown in 2007 when Lewis Hamilton laid down his marker with a stunning, around-the-outside pass of his own team-mate, Fernando Alonso.

Local hero: Australia has an outstanding hero in three-time World Champion Jack Brabham. But, if it's a local driver the Melburnians want, then that's 1980 World Champion Alan Jones. For 2009, they will have just Mark Webber to cheer, from way up the road near Canberra.

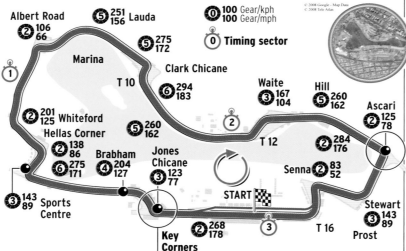

2008 POLE TIME: Hamilton (McLaren),
1m26.714s, 136.795mph/220.150kph
2008 WINNER'S AVERAGE SPEED:
120.930mph/194.618kph

2008 FASTEST LAP: Kovalainen (McLaren),
1m27.418s, 135.704mph/218.395kph
LAP RECORD: M Schumacher (Ferrari),
1m24.125s, 141.016mph/226.933kph, 2004

SEPANG

It's big, it's wide and the climate is humid. However, it ought not be so steamy in 2009, as the Malaysian GP will be held after nightfall for the first time.

It will feel strange, but for the fans at Sepang, the falling of darkness before the start will be a welcome novelty. Not only will it be exciting for them to gain the new experience of watching the cars race in night-time conditions, but it will also be a few degrees cooler, making life easier for everyone at a race that is traditionally held in searing heat and sapping humidity.

By starting at 19:00, the race will follow the trend of being held at a time more convenient for viewers in Europe, meaning a midday start UK time.

The importance of South East Asia to Formula One has been made plain by neighbouring Singapore hosting a grand prix for the first time last year and Sepang's agreement to move its race to an evening start is sure to keep Malaysia on the calendar for years to come.

The Sepang circuit provides more opportunities for overtaking than most thanks to the broad width of its sweeping form, allowing space for drivers to have a go. One of the keys to why it enables passing is that it has a couple of hairpins. The sight of 20 cars trying to get through Turns 1 and 2 together on the opening lap is never less than thrilling, with jousting, passing and repassing. What follows, from Turn 3 to the end of the lap is a wonderful twisting stretch of asphalt, with Turn 12 blindingly fast and the last corner the home of the late braker.

INSIDE TRACK

MALAYSIAN GRAND PRIX

Date:	**5 April**
Circuit name:	**Sepang**
Circuit length:	**3.444 miles/5.542km**
Number of laps:	**56**
Telephone:	**00 60 3 85262000**
Website:	**www.malaysiangp.com.my**

PREVIOUS WINNERS	
1999	**Eddie Irvine** FERRARI
2000	**Michael Schumacher** FERRARI
2001	**Michael Schumacher** FERRARI
2002	**Ralf Schumacher** WILLIAMS
2003	**Kimi Raikkonen** McLAREN
2004	**Michael Schumacher** FERRARI
2005	**Fernando Alonso** RENAULT
2006	**Giancarlo Fisichella** RENAULT
2007	**Fernando Alonso** McLAREN
2008	**Kimi Raikkonen** FERRARI

Most memorable race: Rain can change a race and Ferrari was fastest to react in 2001. Michael Schumacher started ahead of Rubens Barrichello, but a downpour greeted them on lap 2 and both spun off at the same point on lap 3. All those who went past pitted for wet tyres, but Ferrari opted for intermediates. Schumacher had to queue behind Barrichello for his tyres, but then pulled out a superb drive from 11th to victory.

Best for action: The first and last corners are where it's at. When talking of Turn 1, you need to include Turn 2, as the right-hander feeds into it as it doubles back and drops away as it kicks back to the left. Turn 15, is the other main passing opportunity as it's approached by the other long straight down which a car can slipstream into position.

Local hero: Malaysia's only Formula One driver, Alex Yoong, races on in A1GP and sports cars, but his grand prix days are long behind him after he rounded out 2001 and then raced through 2002 for Minardi.

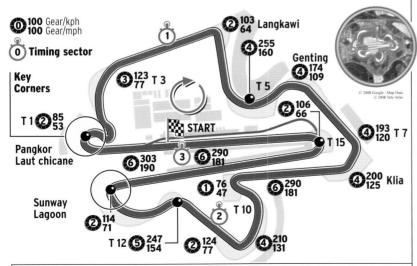

Key Corners

- **0** 100 Gear/kph / 100 Gear/mph
- **0** Timing sector

Corner	Gear	kph/mph
Langkawi	**2**	103 / 64
	4	255 / 160
Genting	**4**	174 / 109
T 3	**3**	123 / 77
T 5		106 / 66 (**2**)
T 1	**2**	85 / 53
T 7	**4**	193 / 120
	6	303 / 190
START	**3**	
	6	290 / 181
Klia	**4**	200 / 125
	1	76 / 47
	6	290 / 181
T 10	**2**	
Pangkor Laut chicane		
Sunway Lagoon	**2**	114 / 71
T 12	**5**	247 / 154
	2	124 / 77
	4	210 / 131
T 15		

© 2008 Google - Map Data
© 2008 Tele Atlas

2008 POLE TIME: **Massa (Ferrari)**, 1m35.748s, 129.490mph/208.394kph
2008 WINNER'S AVERAGE SPEED: **126.768mph/ 204.014kph**

2008 FASTEST LAP: **Heidfeld (BMW Sauber)**, 1m35.366s, 130.045mph/209.288kph
LAP RECORD: **Montoya (Williams)**, 1m34.223s, 131.595mph/211.772kph, 2004

SHANGHAI

Thank goodness Shanghai got its attack in first and cornered China's slice of Formula One's pie, as all the attention was on Beijing and its Olympics in 2008.

China is prone to smog, and so large is the Shanghai International Circuit that on even a half semi-smoggy day it's hard to see the far grandstands at Turn 12, even from the eighth storey wing-shaped bridges over the start/finish straight.

When the Shanghai International Circuit was built for China's Formula One debut in 2004, the teams and personnel were flabbergasted. Not only had the owners built the circuit on thousands of polystyrene blocks in swampy land, but they had made a circuit that dwarfed all others with track and paddock facilities that were second to none.

The circuit, as with all new Formula One tracks, came from the offices of Hermann Tilke, and it's shape bears his mark, particularly the way that it starts. The first corner, well Turns 1 to 3 as they feed directly into each other, is ultra-exciting as a good line into Turn 1 could be the wrong line into Turn 2, with all change again for downhill Turn 3.

The corners are then fast or medium-speed through to Turn 9 where the cars enter a straight up to a sequence of corners not dissimilar to Turns 1 to 3, but in reverse. These spit the cars through a lightly banked bend onto the mile-long straight, down to the all-important hairpin, Turn 13. Once through the final corner, the cars are dwarfed once more by the enormous grandstands and pit buildings.

INSIDE TRACK

CHINESE GRAND PRIX

Date:	**19 April**
Circuit name:	**Shanghai International Circuit**
Circuit length:	**3.390 miles/5.450km**
Number of laps:	**57**
Telephone:	**00 86 2162520000**
Website:	**www.f1china.com.cn**

PREVIOUS WINNERS

2004	**Rubens Barrichello**	FERRARI
2005	**Fernando Alonso**	RENAULT
2006	**Michael Schumacher**	FERRARI
2007	**Kimi Raikkonen**	FERRARI
2008	**Lewis Hamilton**	McLAREN

Most memorable race: The 2007 Chinese GP should have been the race when Lewis Hamilton all but sealed the title, but McLaren kept him out on intermediate tyres that were visibly past their best, waiting for a change in the weather. Then, as he pitted, he slid wide at the pit entry and beached his car in the gravel. He was out and Kimi Raikkonen won for Ferrari to head for the finale with an outside title shot.

Best for action: Turns 1 to 3 blend together and are fantastic on lap 1, but it's Turn 13 at the end of the back straight where the action happens. Braking from 200mph to 50mph and doubling back on oneself is always going to provide the chance for passing, or a collision or a trip straight on up the escape road.

Local hero: Having observed their pride in their Olympians, the Chinese would love one of their own to cheer on, but they're not ready yet. Dutch-born Chinese driver Ho Pin Tung is in GP2 but, apart from a freak second place at Monaco, needs more speed. And there's Cheng Congfu who has been a pacesetter in A1GP.

Local attractions: The city of Shanghai is worth the journey itself and the 1930s' architecture of the Bund on the riverfront in the city centre looks amazing at night as it's topped by illuminated skyscrapers.

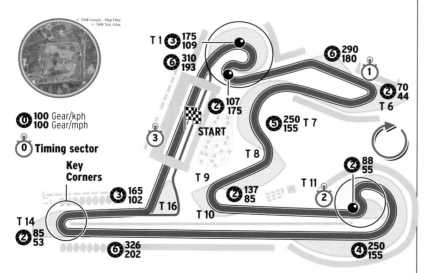

Gear/kph 100 / Gear/mph 100
Timing sector 0
Key Corners

2008 POLE TIME: Lewis Hamilton (McLaren), 1m36.303s, 126.725mph/203.945kph
2008 WINNER'S AVERAGE SPEED: 123.683mph/ 199.049kph

2008 FASTEST LAP: Lewis Hamilton (McLaren), 1m36.325s, 126.587mph/203.722kph
LAP RECORD: M Schumacher (Ferrari), 1m32.238s, 132.202mph/212.759kph, 2004

Lewis Hamilton leading the
Shanghai Grand Prix in 2008.

BAHRAIN

Bahrain brought Formula One to the Gulf, but with a new rival on the block in Abu Dhabi, it finds itself as the older statesman in the region just six years on.

Half a dozen years since Bahrain helds its inaugural grand prix, it still takes some getting used to, as seeing Formula One cars racing against a desert backdrop is about as far away from the traditional verdant scenery around European circuits as it can be. Yet, there they are, with the rocky and dusty desert encircling the circuit, and only the area around the pits and paddock freshened up by heavily-watered grass verges.

Circuit designer Hermann Tilke split the circuit into desert and oasis, with the oasis sector standing out even more with some remarkable architecture, the most notable of which is the 10-storey tower overlooking the first three turns before the track feeds into the desert section.

The circuit at Sakhir has the rare and welcome distinction of offering four lengthy straights leading into tight corners, which certainly allows the drivers to think that they will be able to have a shot at overtaking.

Any driver who has yet to race on the Bahrain International Circuit will expend considerable thought before they travel there on how best to tackle the sequence of bends from Turn 5 to Turn 7, a fast left-right-left sinuous esse. They will also think, no doubt, about how to pull off a passing manoeuvre into the tightish right that is the final corner. After all, it could come in handy on the final lap.

INSIDE TRACK

BAHRAIN GRAND PRIX

Date:	**26 April**
Circuit name:	**Bahrain International Circuit**
Circuit length:	**3.366 miles/5.417km**
Number of laps:	**57**
Telephone:	**00 973 406222**
Website:	**www.bahraingp.com.bh**

PREVIOUS WINNERS

2004	**Michael Schumacher** FERRARI
2005	**Fernando Alonso** RENAULT
2006	**Fernando Alonso** RENAULT 2004
2007	**Felipe Massa** FERRARI
2008	**Felipe Massa** FERRARI

Most memorable race: The most exciting of the five Bahrain GPs was in 2007 when Felipe Massa put a poor start to the season behind him and drove a perfect race to keep his Ferrari ahead of Lewis Hamilton's McLaren, with Kimi Raikkonen having no answers in the second Ferrari and Fernando Alonso's McLaren being beaten to fourth place by BMW Sauber's inspired Nick Heidfeld.

Best for action: Turns 1 and 14, as they're tight corners after long straights and are great for overtaking, although drivers have to be wary of going off line in the braking areas as dust blowing in from the desert can catch them out.

Local hero: As yet, there are no local heroes, no Bahraini drivers at Formula One level, but Salman al Khalifa is honing his craft, spending last year in British Formula Three. The backing will be there to take him to the top, but it's up to the 28-year-old to show he has the talent.

Local attractions: No one would call Bahrain particularly attractive, but if sun, lots of it, sea, there are 236 islands, and sand, well it is a desert, then a holiday alongside the Bahrain GP in this Gulf state could be for you. For a more typical taste of Arabic culture, Bahrain's souk is for people who like to haggle.

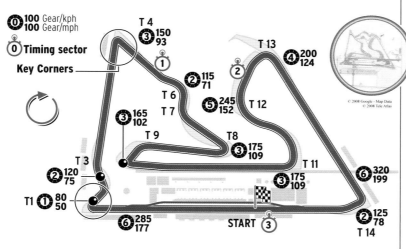

2008 POLE TIME: **Kubica (BMW Sauber)**, 1m33.096s, 130.162mph/209.477kph
2008 WINNER'S AVERAGE SPEED: **126.122mph/ 202.974kph**

2008 FASTEST LAP: **Kovalainen (McLaren)**, 1m33.193s, 129.905mph/209.062kph
LAP RECORD: **M Schumacher (Ferrari)**, 1m30.252s, 134.260mph/216.061kph, 2004

BARCELONA

The debate since Valencia's debut last year is whether this is still Spain's premier venue, especially as races at Barcelona's circuits are rarely festivals of overtaking.

Valencia's street circuit has a grand prix, run under the banner of convenience of the European GP. Yet, for all that, the larger and more dynamic city of Barcelona is the true home of the Spanish GP. Indeed, the Circuit de Catalunya is actually the third circuit linked to the city to have held the race, following Pedralbes in the suburbs which hosted a couple of grands prix in the early 1950s and the circuit in downtown Montjuich Park that was home to the Spanish GP four times between 1969 and 1975. Situated north of the city, the Circuit de Catalunya has been home to the Spanish GP since 1991.

The teams know the circuit extremely well, as they do considerable testing here, not just for the expected mild weather when northern Europe might be cold and wet, but because the lap contains pretty much every type of corner encountered through the series, save for any truly fast ones.

The lap starts with a straight, dipping down to Turns 1 and 2, esses with a gravel trap to collect those who overshoot. The track rises and falls from there before rising again sharply from Turn 7, Wurth, to Campsa at the highest point of the circuit. This has a blind entry and it was here that Heikki Kovalainen ploughed straight into the tyre wall last year. The corner at the bottom end of the back straight, La Caixa, is tight, and the most notable corner of the remainder of the lap is the chicane ahead of the final corner inserted before the 2007 grand prix.

INSIDE TRACK

SPANISH GRAND PRIX

Date:	**10 May**
Circuit name:	**Circuit de Catalunya**
Circuit length:	**2.875 miles/4.627km**
Number of laps:	**65**
Telephone:	**00 34 93 5719771**
Website:	**www.circuitcat.com**

PREVIOUS WINNERS	
1999	**Mika Hakkinen** McLAREN
2000	**Mika Hakkinen** McLAREN
2001	**Michael Schumacher** FERRARI
2002	**Michael Schumacher** FERRARI
2003	**Michael Schumacher** FERRARI
2004	**Michael Schumacher** FERRARI
2005	**Kimi Raikkonen** McLAREN
2006	**Fernando Alonso** RENAULT
2007	**Felipe Massa** FERRARI
2008	**Kimi Raikkonen** FERRARI

Most memorable race: Last year's race wasn't, as there was next to no overtaking. The 1991 grand prix had considerably more, but one of these moves will stand out forever. This was when Nigel Mansell and Ayrton Senna fought wheel-to-wheel down the start/finish straight, with Mansell diving to the inside to grab second. Gerhard Berger kept his lead for only three more laps then pitted. Mansell followed suit a lap later, but hunted him down on rejoining to take a lead he was never to lose.

Best for action: The first corner is the one that provides the best overtaking potential. Elf is approached at 190mph, the entry dipping into this tight right that feeds into Turn 2, with just enough space for an attack either down the inside or, for the brave, around the outside.

Local hero: Three guesses? Yup, it's Fernando Alonso. Sure, he hails from Asturias on the northern coastline, but he's the driver who has single-handedly filled the grandstands at the Circuit de Catalunya. When he won here in 2006, for Renault, the crowd went crazy.

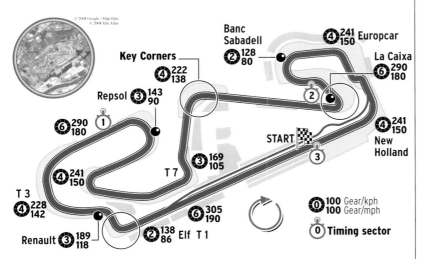

Key Corners — Banc Sabadell · Europcar · La Caixa · Repsol · New Holland · Renault · Elf T1 · START

2008 POLE TIME: **Raikkonen (Ferrari)**, 1m21.813s, 126.508mph/203.595kph
2008 WINNER'S AVERAGE SPEED: **116.454mph/187.415kph**

2008 FASTEST LAP: **Raikkonen (Ferrari)**, 1m21.670s, 127.500mph/205.192kph
LAP RECORD: **Raikkonen (Ferrari)**, 1m21.670s, 127.500mph/205.192kph, 2008

MONACO

With Valencia and Singapore joining the circus last year, Monaco lost its place as Formula One's only street race, but it will never lose its place as the jewel in the crown.

Melbourne's Albert Park encircles a lake. Montreal's Circuit Gilles Villeneuve backs onto one. The new Singapore track runs along its waterfront. Valencia's circuit crosses its yacht basin. Monaco, though, is like no other circuit, it's the pick of the street circuits and its comparison with the harbour in Valencia – made for the America's Cup – is remarkable. In short, the cars in Monaco flash by the platinum standard of yacht collections in the world's most famous harbour.

If the sheer wealth entwined with its obvious history makes it special, the other plus point in Monaco's arsenal is that it has something that almost all grand prix circuits lack: elevation. Combine this with the elegant buildings, the marine backdrops and even the drama of its tunnel, and it offers something that no other circuit can match. Small wonder it's on the must-visit list of every true F1 fan.

It's not all glamour at Monaco, and drivers have to earn their keep in several of the corners. Massenet, at the crest of the hill after the steep climb to Casino Square is not only fast but blind on entry. There are still bumps on the descent to Mirabeau and many drivers are initially spooked by the sixth gear curve in the middle of the tunnel. Braking for the Nouvelle Chicane onto the harbourfront is obviously tricky. Just ask Kimi Raikkonen who lost it there and took out Adrian Sutil last year on what was until then his day of days for Force India.

INSIDE TRACK

MONACO GRAND PRIX

Date:	**24 May**
Circuit name:	**Monte Carlo**
Circuit length:	**2.075 miles/3.339km**
Number of laps:	**78**
Telephone:	**00 377 93152600**
Website:	**www.acm.mc**

PREVIOUS WINNERS

1999	**Michael Schumacher** FERRARI
2000	**David Coulthard** McLAREN
2001	**Michael Schumacher** FERRARI
2002	**David Coulthard** MCLAREN
2003	**Juan Pablo Montoya** WILLIAMS
2004	**Jarno Trulli** RENAULT
2005	**Kimi Raikkonen** McLAREN
2006	**Fernando Alonso** RENAULT
2007	**Fernando Alonso** McLAREN
2008	**Lewis Hamilton** McLAREN

Most memorable race: The 1982 Monaco GP was a race that no-one appeared to want to win, with a mad last few laps when every leader appeared to crash, get a puncture or break down. But the one that stands out in recent years was in 1992 when Nigel Mansell fought back from a delay to harry Ayrton Senna all the way to the finish, all but powering his Williams over the top of the Brazilian's McLaren.

Best for action: The only corner that offers a real chance of a passing move is Ste Devote. Approached by a curving straight, there's just enough room for a driver to have a crack at making a move, with an escape road for drivers who decide to bail out when they realise that they've been just a little too ambitious.

Local hero: Many drivers have based themselves in Monaco for tax reasons, but only two drivers have come from there: Louis Chiron and Olivier Beretta. For now, Monegasques fortunate enough to overlook the circuit will have to make do with cheering for the half of the field they might bump into at the shops.

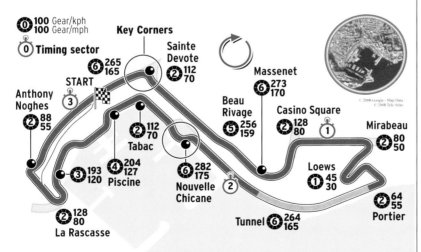

2008 POLE TIME: **Massa (Ferrari), 1m15.787s, 98.566mph/158.626kph**
2008 WINNER'S AVERAGE SPEED: **78.401mph/ 126.174kph**

2008 FASTEST LAP: **Raikkonen (Ferrari), 1m16.689s, 97.424mph/156.789kph**
LAP RECORD: **M Schumacher (Ferrari), 1m14.439s, 100.373mph/161.527kph, 2004**

ISTANBUL

Turkey has one foot in Europe and, more importantly, one in Asia, which is why it proved attractive to Formula One as it looked to increase its global expansion.

Hermann Tilke is, to Formula One, the man with the golden pen. He's the chosen architect for all new grand prix circuits, of which there have been quite a few in the past decade. Turkish race fans can feel delighted too, as the Istanbul Park Circuit is probably his best to date. It's tough to drive, visually appealing and has the added bonus that it offers the possibility of wheel-to-wheel racing with overtaking.

The first corner has echoes of the first corner at Interlagos in Brazil, as it is fairly blind on entry and drops away to the left before arcing right again across the slope through fifth gear Turn 2. In fact, the run from Turn 5 to Turn 7 is also arcing, keeping the drivers right on their toes.

Turn 8 is the one they all fear they will fluff, as it has not one, not two, but three apices. Fortunately for those who get it wrong and spin there, there's an enormous asphalt run-off around its outside to contain their spinning cars. Fractions of a second gained here in qualifying can make or break a driver's weekend.

Turn 9 is sharp and tight, but the one they really have to focus on above all others in the race is Turn 12 at the end of the back straight, as this is where most of the overtaking can be done.

The drivers really have to attack this track and are excited by their rewards. For 2009, now that it's back to a summer date, drivers can expect heat and dust.

INSIDE TRACK

TURKISH GRAND PRIX

Date:	**7 June**
Circuit name:	**Istanbul Park Circuit**
Circuit length:	**3.317 miles/5.338km**
Number of laps:	**58**
Telephone:	**00 90 216 418 5222**
Website:	**www.formula1-istanbul.com**

PREVIOUS WINNERS

2005	**Kimi Raikkonen** McLAREN
2006	**Felipe Massa** FERRARI
2007	**Felipe Massa** FERRARI
2008	**Felipe Massa** FERRARI

Most memorable race: Hermann Tilke did a fine job when he designed the circuit and it has produced some great races. The one in 2006 was the best so far, with Felipe Massa not only scoring his first grand prix win but putting his Ferrari team-mate Michael Schumacher in the shade. The pivotal moment came when the safety car came out when Vitantonio Liuzzi spun and his Toro Rosso blocked the track. Pole-starting Massa was leading and so was first to pit and Schumacher had to queue behind him. This dropped him behind Fernando Alonso's Renault and he was unable to get past again. **Best for action:** Turn 12, at the end of the back straight is where most overtaking takes place, with this second gear left a prime spot for late-braking as the drivers slow their cars from 200mph. Turn 1 also affords a chance to take a look at making a passing manoeuvre. **Local hero;** Turkey is still waiting for one of its own to shine. Jason Tahinci has been their best offering so far, but he failed to deliver in Formula One feeder category GP2. However, this is only the fifth year of Turkey hosting a grand prix and it takes time for interest in Formula One to attract the funding to bring a young talent up the ranks towards the sport's top category.

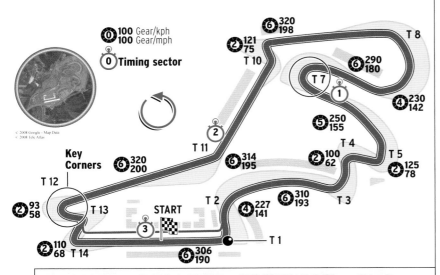

Key Corners

	Gear/kph
100	Gear/mph
0	Timing sector

2008 POLE TIME: Massa (Ferrari), 1m27.617s, 136.289mph/219.336kph

2008 WINNER'S AVERAGE SPEED: 132.882mph/213.853kph

2008 FASTEST LAP: Raikkonen (Ferrari), 1m26.506s, 138.034mph/222.145kph

LAP RECORD: Montoya (McLaren), 1m24.770s, 138.096mph/222.167kph, 2005

SILVERSTONE

The home of British motor racing, host to the first ever World Championship round will be bidding farewell to the British GP this year, having lost the race to Donington.

Silverstone used to alternate with Brands Hatch to host the British GP. That rotation stopped after 1986 and the Northamptonshire circuit has had sole possession of the hosting rights ever since, even though Formula One ringmaster Bernie Ecclestone has long been chiding it for its poor facilities, saying that they need to be upgraded. Certainly, in comparison to the new supercircuits springing up in Shanghai, Bahrain and this year Abu Dhabi, they are less than perfect, but that's down to a complete lack of funding, with none forthcoming from the government.

The main battle has been between Ecclestone and Silverstone's owners, the British Racing Drivers' Club. The breakdown of their contract negotiations was centred on the fact that, although the BRDC had had plans approved to transform the circuit, even building an all-new pit and paddock complex between Club and Abbey, the two parties couldn't agree on money.

And so, like a bolt from the blue at last year's race, Donington Park was given the race from 2010, ending Silverstone's run that started in 1950. Well, 1948, actually in the years before the World Championship began.

One of the greatest shames in this horse-trading has been that Silverstone offers one of the best stretches of asphalt to race on anywhere in the world, with a wonderful flow to its lap, challenging fast corners and many places where an overtaking move needn't be just a fantasy.

INSIDE TRACK

BRITISH GRAND PRIX

Date:	**21 June**
Circuit name:	**Silverstone**
Circuit length:	**3.194 miles/5.140km**
Number of laps:	**60**
Telephone:	**01327 857271**
Website:	**www.silverstone-circuit.co.uk**

PREVIOUS WINNERS

1999	**David Coulthard** McLAREN
2000	**David Coulthard** McLAREN
2001	**Mika Hakkinen** McLAREN
2002	**Michael Schumacher** FERRARI
2003	**Rubens Barrichello** FERRARI
2004	**Michael Schumacher** FERRARI
2005	**Juan Pablo Montoya** McLAREN
2006	**Fernando Alonso** RENAULT
2007	**Kimi Raikkonen** FERRARI
2008	**Lewis Hamilton** McLAREN

Most memorable race: There have been so many at this former airfield that it's hard to choose, but of recent races, the one in 2003 takes some beating. It will be remembered for Rubens Barrichello and Kimi Raikkonen running side-by-side for half a lap before the Brazilian pulled ahead to win for Ferrari in a race that had had its order jumbled by an insane track invader.
Best for action: The best thing about Silverstone is that there are many places to choose between. There's Becketts for watching the cars at their most spectacular, Stowe for overtaking, Abbey for attempted overtaking and Copse for action on lap 1. In balance, Stowe is the best, especially as the grandstands there afford a clear view of the cars as they come down the Hangar Straight, try their moves into Stowe and try again through the Vale or out of Club,
Local hero: For a long time it was Nigel Mansell, then it was Damon Hill, David Coulthard and most recently Jenson Button. But now it's Lewis Hamilton, as since 2007 he has added tens of thousands to the gate.

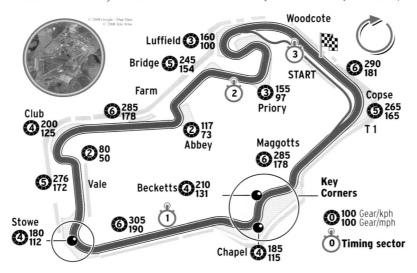

2008 POLE TIME: Kovalainen (McLaren), 1m21.049s, 141.870mph/228.318kph
2008 WINNER'S AVERAGE SPEED: 115.938mph/ 186.584kph

2008 FASTEST LAP: Raikkonen (Ferrari), 1m32.150s, 124.797mph/200.842kph
LAP RECORD: **M Schumacher (Ferrari),** 1m18.739s, 146.059mph/235.048kph, 2004

NURBURGRING

The alternation with Hockenheim continues for the right to host the German GP and its totally different character is sure to produce a totally different race.

The era of German domination of Formula One came to an end when Michael Schumacher retired at the end of the 2006 season. However, BMW's involvement and Mercedes' partnership with McLaren, the fact that Toyota is based in Cologne and that five of last year's drivers were German mean that the country has considerable interest in its home grand prix. This year, it's the Nurburgring's turn to host the race and the hilltop circuit is ready to greet the grand prix teams with its mixture of middle-speed corners and its inimitable, changeable weather.

Opened in 1984 after being built over a fraction of the original and much feared 14-mile Nurburgring Nordschleife, the circuit now feels very much part of the establishment, with its packed campsite – the Germans love to camp – and raucous, air horn-wielding spectators very much part of the package.

The first corner is far tighter than it used to be, as a wide hairpin that encourages overtaking, then it feeds into a long left-hander followed by a tighter, slightly banked one and a sharp right. The track has gradient and drops to a hairpin, the Dunlop Kehre, before climbing back to Michelin Kurve then dropping into the fast back section with its tight chicane from which the Nordschleife can be spotted snaking out into the surrounding forests.

There might be more races at the Nurburgring in the future, as financial problems being experienced by Hockenheim may lead to the breakdown of the German GP's alternation.

INSIDE TRACK

GERMAN GRAND PRIX

Date:	**12 July**
Circuit name:	**Nurburgring**
Circuit length:	**3.199 miles/5.148km**
Number of laps:	**60**
Telephone:	**00 49 2691 923060**
Website:	**www.nuerburgring.de**

PREVIOUS WINNERS

1998*	**Mika Hakkinen** McLAREN
1999**	**Johnny Herbert** STEWART
2000**	**Michael Schumacher** FERRARI
2001**	**Michael Schumacher** FERRARI
2002**	**Rubens Barrichello** FERRARI
2003**	**Ralf Schumacher** WILLIAMS
2004**	**Michael Schumacher** FERRARI
2005**	**Fernando Alonso** RENAULT
2006**	**Michael Schumacher** FERRARI
2007**	**Fernando Alonso** McLAREN

* As Luxemburg GP ** As European GP

Most memorable race: For sheer mad, tospy-turvy action, 1999 had it all. Heinz-Harald Frentzen led from pole for Jordan before electrical failure hit as he left his pit stop. McLaren's David Coulthard took over, then rain fell and he spun off, giving Williams racer Ralf Schumacher the lead. He pitted and Giancarlo Fisichella led for Benetton, but spun off. Now it was Johnny Herbert's turn as track conditions changed again and he gave Stewart its one and only win, thanking his decision to go for full wets at his first stop, just as the rain arrived.

Best for action: The first corner has its share of incident, but the Dunlop Kehre has seen some pure overtaking moves, with one that Juan Pablo Montoya pulled on Michael Schumacher in 2003 standing out as he went around the outside...

Local hero: It seemed impossible to replace Michael Schumacher, the driver who gave Germans everything they had been looking for since Formula One began, but Sebastian Vettel is the name on their lips since his win at Monza.

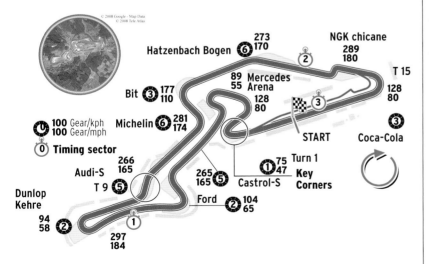

2007 POLE TIME: **Raikkonen (Ferrari),** 1m31.450s, 125.931mph/202.667kph
2007 WINNER'S AVERAGE SPEED: **91.091mph/ 146.597kph**

2007 FASTEST LAP: **Massa (Ferrari),** 1m32.853s, 124.046mph/199.633kph
LAP RECORD: **M Schumacher (Ferrari),** 1m29.468s, 128.721mph/207.157kph, 2004

HUNGARORING

Only exceptional circumstance or changes in weather conditions contrive to make this race a cracker, as the circuit layout all but mitigates against overtaking.

It seems just a few years ago that Hungary joined the grand prix circus, breaking new ground as Formula One went behind the Iron Curtain. Amazingly, that was 23 years ago, firmly making it part of the establishment.

Unlike certain more traditional and long-standing grand prix circuits in Europe, the Hungaroring can feel secure of its future, as a contract extension until 2016 was signed last year.

The circuit itself is wonderful for viewing but truly terrible for racing, with its races invariably processional. The cars do look spectacular here, bouncing off kerbs, with low camera angles adding the impression of speed to what is in fact only a medium-speed circuit.

To drive, the circuit is a challenge, with constant changes of gradient making it more interesting than most. However, the real need for precision is that the majority of corners lead almost straight into the next one, and so getting slightly off line will have obvious consequences.

The track runs alongside one side of a valley, drops away through Turns 1 and 2 into the dip then rises up the other side through fourth gear Turn 4 and runs along in front of the spectator banking on the far side of the valley to Turn 11 before diving back to the valley floor again, then up the climb through Turns 12 to 14 to return to the start/finish straight.

INSIDE TRACK

HUNGARIAN GRAND PRIX

Date:	26 July
Circuit name:	Hungaroring
Circuit length:	2.722 miles/4.381km
Number of laps:	70
Telephone:	00 36 2 844 1861
Website:	www.hungaroring.hu

PREVIOUS WINNERS

1999	**Mika Hakkinen** McLAREN
2000	**Mika Hakkinen** McLAREN
2001	**Michael Schumacher** FERRARI
2002	**Rubens Barrichello** FERRARI
2003	**Fernando Alonso** RENAULT
2004	**Michael Schumacher** FERRARI
2005	**Kimi Raikkonen** McLAREN
2006	**Jenson Button** HONDA
2007	**Lewis Hamilton** McLAREN
2008	**Heikki Kovalainen** McLAREN

Most memorable race: Michael Schumacher produced some astonishing drives, but his drive to victory here in 1998 was one of the most remarkable. To put one over the McLarens that had qualified on the front row, he had to run a three-stop strategy, being instructed by Ferrari mastermind Ross Brawn to run every lap as though it was a qualifying lap. And this he did, getting ahead of Mika Hakkinen and David Coulthard after their second stops and doing enough to still be ahead after his third.

Best for action: It has to be Turn 1, as there is little to no chance at any of the 13 other corners, unless the driver in front makes a mistake. Felipe Massa proved last year that you can attack around the outside here and make it stick.

Local hero: This is a hard one, as there has only been one Hungarian driver in Formula One, Zsolt Baumgartner, and he failed to shine. However, the Hungaroring is always packed with Finns and now Poles, as it's their closest grand prix to home. The Finns have a language linked to Magyar, so feel some extra allegiance.

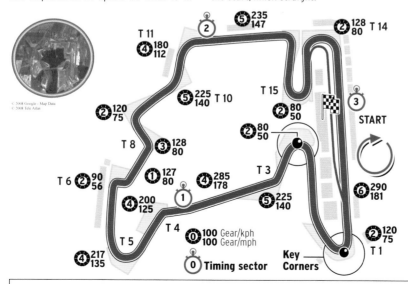

2008 POLE TIME: **Hamilton (McLaren),** 1m20.899s, 121.129mph/194.938kph
2008 WINNER'S AVERAGE SPEED: **117.308mph/ 188.790kph**

2008 FASTEST LAP: **Raikkonen (Ferrari),** 1m21.195s, 120.697mph/194.243kph
LAP RECORD: **M Schumacher (Ferrari),** 1m19.071s, 123.828mph/199.461kph, 2004

VALENCIA

For so long, Monaco was street racing for Formula One. Then, like buses, along came two new street tracks in '08, with Valencia the less appealing of the newcomers.

Monaco is ancient, regal and louche. Valencia is a brash newcomer, its wealth from agriculture and industry rather than simply arriving with incomers looking to play the roulette tables and make the most of a lenient tax regime.

Another great difference is that the Monaco track clings to the gradient of the slopes of Monte Carlo. The Valencia street circuit has no gradient at all. There are yachts in both harbours, but only the ones in Valencia look as though their choice is to be powered by wind.

Of the track itself, the Valencia circuit has one notable straight, which is one more than Monaco. This, of course, encourages overtaking at its end, giving it a clear advantage over Monaco.

As with any street circuit, there are more bumps than on purpose-built circuits, and the first proper corner, Turn 2, is made all the trickier by being bumpy as well as tight. The next stretch of the lap is a little stop-start in nature down to Turn 8, making it clear how the engineers need to find a balance between aerodynamic balance and traction.

Then comes the circuit's trademark feature, the bridge, and getting a good exit through the tight right-hander off it is vital, as it opens onto the circuit's longest straight down to Turn 12. Turns 17 and 25 are also both tight and are sure to produce incident again.

INSIDE TRACK

EUROPEAN GRAND PRIX

Date:	**23 August**
Circuit name:	**Valencia**
Circuit length:	**3.401 miles/5.473km**
Number of laps:	**57**
Telephone:	**00 34 963164007**
Website:	**www.valenciastreetcircuit.com**

PREVIOUS WINNERS

2008	**Felipe Massa** FERRARI

Most memorable race: Last year's grand prix, the first on the Valencia street circuit, provided a less than exciting debut as Felipe Massa simply dominated proceedings.

Best for action: Last year's inaugural race showed that Turn 2 is where the best of the action happens, and this will be on the opening lap, when the field is bunched.

Local hero: The Spaniards always felt Europe's poor neighbours when it came to success in Formula One. Alfonso de Portago hinted at great things in the 1950s, but died in a crash on the Mille Miglia. Then, despite Pedro de la Rosa's best efforts in the 1990s, there was no likely race winner until Fernando Alonso came along with Renault. He remains the nation's big hope, but having two grands prix within its borders means that more may be backed to follow.

Local attractions: The city of Valencia made a massive push to promote itself when it landed the deal to host the America's Cup yachting gala in 2007. The construction of a marina tidied up the waterfront and adding the European GP brought yet more people to the city, as well as finding a use for a defunct railway yard.

Who designed it: Leading circuit architect Hermann Tilke was of course the man given the task and he very much enjoyed working on a street circuit, making the most of what was already there in the urban landscape.

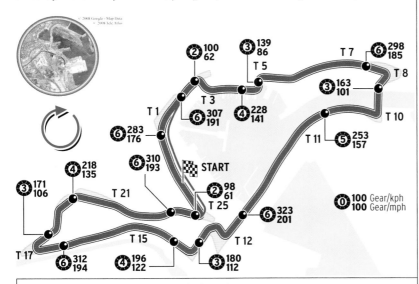

POLE TIME 2008: **Massa (Ferrari), 1m38.989s/ 123.686mph/199.054kph**
2008 WINNER'S AVERAGE SPEED: **120.560mph/ 194.023kph**

2008 FASTEST LAP: **Massa (Ferrari), 1m38.708s, 124.039mph/199.621kph, 2008**
LAP RECORD: **Massa (Ferrari), 1m38.708s, 124.039mph/199.621kph, 2008**

SPA-FRANCORCHAMPS

This magnificent strip of tarmac through a forest has all a racing circuit should have: fast and slow corners, changes of gradient and, always, the chance of rain.

Monaco has it. Silverstone has it. Monza has it. So does Spa-Francorchamps: history in its every curve, memories galore and magnificence in its patina. This Belgian circuit retains the closest links with a road racing past, although the 9.2-mile lap has long been pruned to 4.3, albeit keeping its use of terrain to define its character.

For the drivers, it provides a stern test. For the strategists, it provides a nightmare as the weather in the Ardennes uplands is capricious. When the original circuit that embraced the neighbouring valley beyond Les Combes was used, it could be bone dry in the pits yet pouring at the far end of the track. Even today, the weather is extremely localized and rain a potent threat.

For all the changes to the pits and paddock, the playing surface is largely unchanged. La Source is still tight enough to catch out a few on the opening lap. Eau Rouge at the foot of the hill that follows is still a test as it's taken in sixth, with the ground rearing up in the drivers' faces as they pile into Raidillion. The straight from here is long and kinked.

From Les Combes, it's then downhill all the way through the fast and tricky Pouhon to Stavelot, where the original circuit is rejoined for the ascent to the pits. Blanchimont is still a corner of note, at sixth gear through the trees, before the still unsatisfactory final corner where the Bus Stop double chicane used to be.

INSIDE TRACK

BELGIAN GRAND PRIX

Date:	**13 September**
Circuit name:	**Spa-Francorchamps**
Circuit length:	**4.352 miles/7.004km**
Number of laps:	**44**
Telephone:	**00 32 8727 5138**
Website:	**www.spa-francorchamps.be**

PREVIOUS WINNERS

1997	**Michael Schumacher** FERRARI
1998	**Damon Hill** JORDAN
1999	**David Coulthard** McLAREN
2000	**Mika Hakkinen** McLAREN
2001	**Michael Schumacher** FERRARI
2002	**Michael Schumacher** FERRARI
2004	**Kimi Raikkonen** McLAREN
2005	**Kimi Raikkonen** McLAREN
2007	**Kimi Raikkonen** FERRARI
2008	**Felipe Massa** FERRARI

Most memorable race: Michael Schumacher's first win, in 1992, was a wild one. The weather had a role to play, but even that wasn't expected to slow the progress of Nigel Mansell and Williams. Ayrton Senna led lap 1 before Mansell and Riccardo Patrese moved past. Then rain arrived and they pitted, except for Senna, but Mansell soon resumed control. What would be key as it dried was when to change back to slicks, and Schumacher lucked in here. He ran off the track and rejoined behind Benetton team-mate Martin Brundle, noticed his tyres were blistering and pitted. It proved to be the optimum moment.

Best for action: Les Combes is one of the key overtaking points as drivers slow for the right-left flick. Pop through the tunnel there, and you can then see down the hill to Pouhon.

Local hero: Jacky Ickx came close to the 1970 world title. Thierry Boutsen did his best in the 1980s, but since then the cupboard has been bare. Fortunately, the circuit's central location makes it easy to reach for British, French and German fans to cheer on their own.

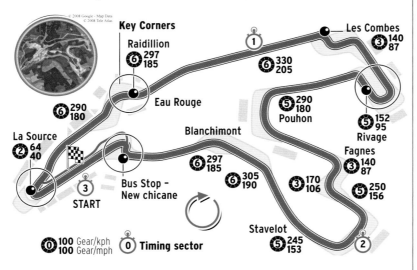

2008 POLE TIME: **Hamilton (McLaren)**, 1m47.338s, 145.961mph/234.902kph
2008 WINNER'S AVERAGE SPEED: **138.417mph/222.761kph**

2008 FASTEST LAP: **Raikkonen (Ferrari)**, 1m47.930s, 145.163mph/233.618kph
LAP RECORD: Raikkonen (Ferrari), 1m47.930s, 145.161mph/233.614kph, 2008

MONZA

This great Italian circuit is one of the remaining high temples of motorsport, one of the few places where the past and present are linked with a shared spirit.

For all the splendour of the supercircuits built in the past decade, lavished with government money to bring a country to Formula One's high table, this famous Italian circuit has something that they can never be born with. It has character.

It has history aplenty too, having been open for racing since 1922, but its very nature as a flat-out racing circuit is what really defines it.

The two banked corners have long since been taken over by weeds and the insertion in 1972 of three chicanes ended the battles of slipstreaming packs of cars, but the spirit of Monza lives on.

Sure, the first chicane, a tight right-left, bunches the cars and if braking is left a fraction too late by the chasing car it can lead to contact or a trip over the kerbs, but it does provide overtaking potential. The chicane's existence, though, slows the cars through the Curva Grande, a fifth gear right before the second chicane. This is the Variante della Roggia.

Next up, the Lesmos are tricky, with a good exit from the second important for the blast back under the old circuit down to Variante Ascari.

After this third chicane, there's a straight then the final corner. But what a final corner: Parabolica, out of which the highest exit speed possible is essential to stand a chance of overtaking at the end of the long start/finish straight.

INSIDE TRACK

ITALIAN GRAND PRIX

Date:	**6 September**
Circuit name:	**Monza**
Circuit length:	**3.600 miles/5.793km**
Number of laps:	**53**
Telephone:	**00 39 39 24821**
Website:	**www.monzanet.it**

PREVIOUS WINNERS

1999	**Heinz-Harald Frentzen** JORDAN
2000	**Michael Schumacher** FERRARI
2001	**Juan Pablo Montoya** WILLIAMS
2002	**Rubens Barrichello** FERRARI
2003	**Michael Schumacher** FERRARI
2004	**Rubens Barrichello** FERRARI
2005	**Juan Pablo Montoya** McLAREN
2006	**Michael Schumacher** FERRARI
2007	**Fernando Alonso** McLAREN
2008	**Sebastian Vettel** TORO ROSSO

Most memorable race: When it comes to exciting grands prix, none can match what Italian fans enjoyed in 1971, with the first five drivers home covered by just 0.61s. That it ended with a first-time winner made it all the more exciting. Chris Amon had started from pole for Matra, but he pulled off his visor and had to slow. This left a five-car pack changing position at every corner. Ronnie Peterson led into the final corner, but braked too late and Francois Cevert dived to pass him, only to find Peter Gethin's BRM diving inside him. Gethin nosed ahead and just held off Peterson to the flag. The gap was 0.01s, with Cevert third and Mike Hailwood fourth and Gethin's team-mate Howden Ganley fifth.
Best for action: The first and second chicanes are where the overtaking happens on lap 1, but thereafter it's the first chicane that offers place changes after the sprint from the Parabolica.
Local hero: Giancarlo Fisichella has carried the honour of Italy for the past decade, but the tifosi will have to look to a rising star if they want one of their own in a Ferrari.

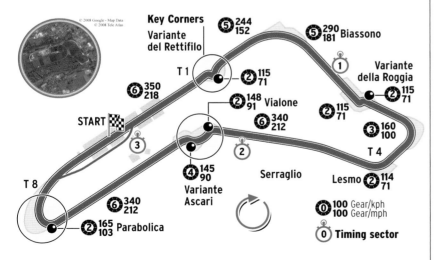

Key Corners

Variante del Rettifilo · T 1 · ⑤ 244/152 · ② 115/71 · ⑥ 350/218 · START · ③ · ⑤ 290/181 Biassono · ① · Variante della Roggia · ② 115/71 · ② 148/91 Vialone · ⑥ 340/212 · ② 115/71 · ③ 160/100 · T 4 · ② · Serraglio · Lesmo ② 114/71 · T 8 · ④ 145/90 Variante Ascari · ⑥ 340/212 · ② 165/103 Parabolica

⓪ 100/100 Gear/kph Gear/mph

⓪ **Timing sector**

2008 POLE TIME: **Vettel (Toro Rosso)**, 1m37.535s, 132.875mph/213.843kph
2008 WINNER'S AVERAGE SPEED: **131.814mph/212.134kph**

2008 FASTEST LAP: **Raikkonen (Ferrari)**, 1m28.047s, 147.194mph/236.886kph
LAP RECORD: **Barrichello (Ferrari)**, 1m21.046s, 159.899mph/257.321kph, 2004

Former World Champion Fernando Alonso
recorded his win since returning to Renault
at Singapore in 2008.

SINGAPORE

Singapore's street circuit broke new ground last year, not only for taking Formula One to a different country, but famously for holding its first night race.

No one who watched last year's Singapore GP will forget the images of cars blasting past the illuminated city skyline. Night racing is here to stay, being not only spectacular but greatly desired by Bernie Ecclestone as it means fans in Europe no longer need to rise in the early hours to catch the action. That the racing is held in one of South-East Asia's most powerful commercial hubs makes the event even more important in Ecclestone's eyes.

This wonderful street race facility offers something unusual to Formula One: it runs anti-clockwise, like only Istanbul and Interlagos. Bearing the hallmark of circuit architect Hermann Tilke, the first corner is tight, and followed immediately by a right and a left to ensure that there is changing of position on lap 1.

The next section streaks past the banks before turning right onto Raffles Boulevard, ducking through an underpass at 200mph. A sequence of 90 degree bends then a short straight follows, before the cars race past the colonial government buildings.

There has never been a feature like it in Formula One, so the arched Anderson Bridge is extremely distinctive and loved by photographers, but not so by drivers looking to overtake as it's so narrow.

The home stretch crosses the Esplanade Bridge, takes a sharp right then squirms beneath a grandstand before feeding into the fast left that's the final corner.

INSIDE TRACK

SINGAPORE GRAND PRIX

Date:	27 September
Circuit name:	Singapore
Circuit length:	3.148 miles/5.067km
Number of laps:	61
Telephone:	00 65 67315900
Website:	www.singaporegp.sg

PREVIOUS WINNERS

2008	**Fernando Alonso** RENAULT

Most memorable race: Well, as last year's race was the first, it has to be that one... The moment that stands out from 2008 was the sight of the start of F1's first ever night race as Massa led the pack down to the first corner.

Best for action: The 90-degree left at Turn 7, approached down the circuit's longest straight proved to be the best place for overtaking.

Local hero: Singapore has a population of just 3.6 million and no race circuit until now, apart from a rough-and-ready street circuit for club racing in the 1960s, so it's not surprising that it hasn't produced a driver of note yet. Dennis Lian is the best qualified native-born driver so far, but the chances of a home-grown star reaching F1 rests with the next generation.

Local attractions: Think Singapore and many think of Raffles, the landmark hotel where visitors are expected to kick back in a raffia chair and sip Singapore Slings. There is so much besides in this immaculate 'city of the lion', with some stunning modern architecture in the central business district that tower over the old British colonial buildings..

Who designed it: Circuit designer Hermann Tilke knew the boundaries within which the circuit would be contained, as street circuits are always bound in by buildings, roads or other physical features. He used the shape well, with the trip across the water on the Anderson and Esplanade bridges adding to its distinctive nature.

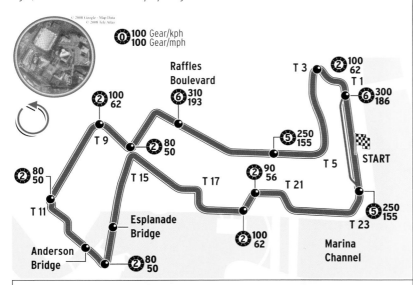

© 2008 Google - Map Data
© 2008 Tele Atlas

0 100 Gear/kph
100 Gear/mph

Raffles Boulevard

6 310 / 193

2 100 / 62

T 9

2 80 / 50

T 15

2 80 / 50

T 11

T 17

Anderson Bridge

2 80 / 50

Esplanade Bridge

T 3 **2** 100 / 62

T 1

6 300 / 186

5 250 / 155

T 5 START

2 90 / 56

T 21

2 100 / 62

5 250 / 155

T 23

Marina Channel

2008 POLE TIME: **Massa (Ferrari), 1m44.801s, 108.136mph/174.029kph**

2008 WINNER'S AVERAGE SPEED: **98.219mph/158.068kph**

2008 FASTEST LAP: **Raikkonen (Ferrari), 1m45.599s, 107.358mph/172.776kph**

LAP RECORD: **Raikkonen (Ferrari), 1m45.599s, 107.358mph/172.776kph, 2008**

SUZUKA

Formula One has missed this great circuit since Fuji wrested the race away in 2007, but an alternation has now started so Suzuka will be a biennial treat.

One of the best pieces of news for 2009 is that Suzuka is back, starting its alternation with Fuji Speedway, as it is one of the true tests for today's drivers.

The reason that Suzuka has been brought back in from the cold is that it's owned by Honda, a manufacturer extremely important to Formula One. Fuji Speedway is owned by Toyota, so the alternation makes perfect commercial sense.

The circuits could hardly be more different, though, with the only similarity being that they are on hillside locations.

Suzuka, which hosted grands prix from 1987 when Gerhard Berger won for Ferrari to 2006 when Fernando Alonso was first home for Renault, is a far more challenging

proposition. Even the first two corners, which look tame enough on the circuit plan have an awkward camber.

From this the lowest part of the circuit, the track climbs through the magnificent double esses before cresting the slope at Dunlop Curve. Unusually, the circuit dips under itself and feeds up to its only hairpin. Then it climbs again through a long right to Spoon Curve that seems to keep turning left forever before feeding the cars down a long straight. The toughest corner is next, 130R, a 170mph left that is less spooky since the crash barriers were moved back a few years ago. The lap is completed by a chicane and turns downhill again through Last Corner onto the start/finish straight.

INSIDE TRACK

JAPANESE GRAND PRIX

Date:	**4 October**
Circuit name:	**Suzuka**
Circuit length:	**3.608 miles/5.806km**
Number of laps:	**53**
Telephone:	**00 81 593 783620**
Website:	**www.suzukacircuit.co.jp**

PREVIOUS WINNERS	
2003	**Rubens Barrichello** FERRARI
2004	**Michael Schumacher** FERRARI
2005	**Kimi Raikkonen** McLAREN
2006	**Fernando Alonso** RENAULT

Most memorable race: One of the finest drives at Suzuka was Damon Hill's in atrocious conditions in 1994. It was the penultimate race of the series and he had to win to stay in touch with Michael Schumacher. Heavy rain made the start dangerous and the safety car was brought out after four laps following a crash on the main straight. Schumacher led from Hill, but the race was red-flagged after Martin Brundle hit a marshal attending another incident. On resumption, Hill took the lead when Schumacher pitted and drove a blinder to keep ahead to the finish.

Best for action: For spectacle, the esses have few peers, as a driver on a flying lap will find a flow despite having to make rapid changes of direction. For overtaking, the vantage point has to be the Casio Triangle, the final sequence of corners. A tight right over the crest of a hill followed immediately by a tight left offers drivers the chance to make a move, especially if they've had a good run through 130R.

Local hero: Japan has yet to produce a grand prix winner and that rankles with the Japanese fans. Aguri Suzuki was on the podium here for Larrousse in 1990 and Takuma Sato also took a third place finish at Indianapolis for BAR in 2004 but, for now, they will have to hope that Kazuki Nakajima continues to improve.

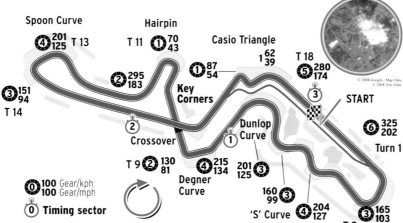

2006 POLE TIME: **Massa (Ferrari), 1m29.599s, 144.977mph/233.319kph**
2006 WINNER'S AVERAGE SPEED: **136.690MPH/219.982KPH**

2008 FASTEST LAP: **Alonso (Renault), 1m32.676s, 140.164mph/225.572kph**
LAP RECORD: **Raikkonen (McLaren), 1m31.540s, 141.904mph/228.372kph, 2005**

INTERLAGOS

South Americans really love Formula One and this is their only chance to see it live. Interlagos is still rather rough around the edges, but it has a real heart to it.

The images that Formula One ringmaster Bernie Ecclestone wants beamed around the globe include packed grandstands, great racing and all the corporate hoardings bathed in sunshine. Brazil provides this, and so much more, as the unadulterated passion of its fans allied with the spectacular setting ticks all the boxes. It's not a modern, pristine facility like Shanghai, Istanbul or Sepang, rather a warts-and-all circuit. It's also Formula One's only foothold in South America and so gains even more clout when the sport is pitched at sponsors. And now its contract has been extended to 2015 so new pits and paddock will be built.

Although cut from its original 4.9-mile length in 1990, the 2.6-mile lap is still more than enough of a challenge. The first corner, the Senna S, is at the crest of a slope and the track drops away to the left, arcing immediately to the right before aping the outline of the original track on the drop towards the lakes that pepper the bottom half of the circuit's land. From here, Interlagos climbs and drops down the slopes of the hill behind the paddock, with bumps appearing every year to catch the drivers out through corners such as Ferra Dura, Mergulho and Laranja. It's out of Juncao that drivers must excel, though, as this is where they must have maximum traction on exit as they hit the uphill, ever-curving start/finish 'straight'.

INSIDE TRACK

BRAZILIAN GRAND PRIX

Date:	**1 November**
Circuit name:	**Interlagos**
Circuit length:	**2.667 miles/4.292km**
Number of laps:	**71**
Telephone:	**00 55 11 813 5775**
Website:	**www.interlagos.com**

PREVIOUS WINNERS

1999	**Mika Hakkinen** McLAREN
2000	**Michael Schumacher** FERRARI
2001	**David Coulthard** McLAREN
2002	**Michael Schumacher** FERRARI
2003	**Giancarlo Fisichella** JORDAN
2004	**Juan Pablo Montoya** WILLIAMS
2005	**Juan Pablo Montoya** McLAREN
2006	**Felipe Massa** FERRARI
2007	**Kimi Raikkonen** FERRARI
2008	**Felipe Massa** FERRARI

Most memorable race: The 2007 race was the one in which Lewis Hamilton arrived with a four-point lead over McLaren team-mate Fernando Alonso and yet Kimi Raikkonen out-stripped them both to win the title for Ferrari. Hamilton tripped over Raikkonen at the start and fell to fourth. Two corners later, he locked up and dropped to eighth. With Massa leading, he had to be sure of fifth and soon reached that, only to slow with a gearbox problem. He made it back to seventh, but Raikkonen's win landed the Finn the crown.

Best for action: Drivers reach Descida do Lago, the lowest point in the circuit, anxious to make a move. Trouble is, it can be slippery offline into this negative camber corner.

Local hero: Ayrton Senna was a hero to all Brazilians. Replacing him is impossible, but having a second Senna, nephew Bruno, in Formula One will keep them happy. The fans' support makes the grandstands around the top half of Interlagos feel like a coliseum and no Brazilian driver can fail to feel their support.

Key Corners

- ⓪ Timing sector
- **100** Gear/kph / **100** Gear/mph

- Senna S T 1 — ② 88/55
- ⑥ 290/180
- **START** ③
- Arquibancadas — ⑥ 270/168 T 15
- ④ 185/115 — Ferra dura
- ① 93/58 — T 8
- ④ 244/152
- Pinheirinho
- ③ 148/92 T 2
- Mergulho — ③ 235/146
- ⑤ 275/171
- ① 74/46 — Bico do Pato — T 12
- ② 201/125 — Curva do Sol
- Reta Oposta — ⑥ 290/180
- ④ 245/152
- ② (2)
- ③ 177/110 — Junçao
- ① (1)
- Descida do Lago ③ 143/89

© 2008 Google - Map Data
© 2008 Tele Atlas

2008 POLE TIME: Massa (Ferrari), 1m12.368s, 133.169mph/214.316kph
2008 WINNER'S AVERAGE SPEED: 120.947mph/194.646kph

2008 FASTEST LAP: Massa (Ferrari), 1m13.736s, 130.722mph/210.377kph
LAP RECORD: Montoya (Williams), 1m11.473s, 134.837mph/217.000kph

ABU DHABI

Abu Dhabi is hoping that the best has been saved for last as its inaugural grand prix will bring the season to a close in an opulent new waterfront setting.

When is a circuit not a circuit? When it's been built from scratch, almost regardless of expense by an oil-rich Arab sheikhdom, because then it will be a circuit plus a marina plus a Ferrari theme park, hotels, apartments and no doubt supercar showrooms alongside its exclusive shopping mall.

Dubai has become the home for almost all sport in the Middle East, but Bahrain pulled off a coup by landing the first grand prix on the Arabian Peninsula and now Abu Dhabi, capital of the United Arab Emirates, has also put one over its brash neighbour Dubai.

Abu Dhabi's Yas Island is the venue for this new circuit and it looks amazing, with its layout of appreciable straights and 20 corners forming an interesting shape, with the chicane then hairpin sequence of Turns 5 to 7 being right beneath huge grandstands. Another likely spot for overtaking is at the end of the long main straight, again with a grandstand sited to witness the action through Turns 8 and 9. Turn 11, at the end of an arcing straight, also ought to provide some fireworks.

Computer simulations suggest that the cars will top 200mph, with a predicted lap speed of 1m38s.

If you want to get a feeling for the circuit ahead of the event, click on the animated circuit tour on the official website – www.abudhabigp.com.

INSIDE TRACK

ABU DHABI GRAND PRIX

Date:	**15 November**
Circuit name:	**Abu Dhabi**
Circuit length:	**3.429 miles/5.518km**
Number of laps:	**56**
Telephone:	**00 971 4 366 2125**
Website:	**www.abudhabigp.com**

Most memorable race: This is still to come...

Best for action: Turn 8, at the end of the longest straight will be the most likely spot for overtaking, while Turn 1 looks tight enough to cause a few problems on the opening lap.

Local hero: None, as yet, but there are a host of drivers from the United Arab Emirates advancing through the junior formulae.

Local attractions: With golf courses, a water park, polo fields and marinas as well as the hotels, restaurants and shopping, there's probably no need to leave Yas Island, which is just how the developers would like it. The prime attraction to adrenaline-fuelled visitors will certainly be the Ferrari theme park, with its 70m high G Force Tower sure to be its must-do ride. There will also be a twin rollercoaster so that friends can race against each other. The remainder of the capital of the UAE deserves a visit, though, as the largest of the seven emirates, with welcome winter sunshine assured along its wide corniche and tree-lined boulevards. The Al Meena District is the place to go for more traditional Arabic souks, with the Madinat Zayed souk for those looking to buy gold. The Heritage Village on the seafront offers a look into Abu Dhabi's Bedouin past.

Who designed it: Hermann Tilke is the man who was let loose on crafting a circuit from this 2550 hectare island to the east of Abu Dhabi Island, with golf courses adding some welcome green from the yellow and brown desert hues. He has split the circuit into three distinct sectors: a high-speed section, a street section and then a marina section to complete the lap.

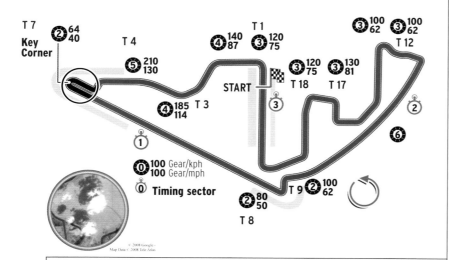

ABU DHABI 2009

The new purpose-built Abu Dhabi circuit has been rewarded with the opportunity to host the 2009 season finale.

REVIEW OF THE 2008 SEASON

Last season offered considerable interest even before it reached its nail-biting conclusion when Lewis Hamilton pipped Felipe Massa to the title in the dying seconds. Yet it wasn't all Ferrari and McLaren, with Renault, BMW Sauber and the fast-changing Toro Rosso also taking wins as they advanced from the midfield. Two new circuits made a splash, but it was the night race in Singapore that stood out.

The spectacular images of a floodlit circuit picked out as it weaved its way between Singapore's waterfront and city backdrop during Formula One's first night race were amazing. However, the most memorable image of 2008 was Felipe Massa's forlorn, tear-stained expression as he mounted the podium in front of his adoring fans after that outstanding finale in Brazil. To be beaten to the title was one thing, but for it to have been taken away just when it was

finally, surely, his was cruel beyond belief. Don't let anyone tell you that raw emotion has no place in top-line sport. It does.

Sure, the season was a battle royal between Ferrari and McLaren, as it has been so many times before, but the fact that BMW Sauber sat right on their tails made things interesting. Overtaking was as hard as ever, but Robert Kubica and Nick Heidfeld were there to pick up the pieces when they stumbled. Indeed, Kubica might have

lucked into victory in Canada – a first both for he and his team – when Hamilton made a mess of things, but it even put him into the lead of the drivers' championship mid-season.

There was ebb and flow all season between Ferrari and McLaren. In fact, that should read between Massa and Hamilton, as reigning World Champion Kimi Raikkonen couldn't get his Ferrari to work in qualifying, while things seldom went right for Heikki Kovalainen in the second McLaren and he failed to match Hamilton. Some drivers were hampered by traction control having been banned, but the early-season rash of accidents soon dried up.

Both of the top teams made mistakes, most notably Ferrari during pit stops, but McLaren seemed to take the brunt of rulings from the stewards who stepped in increasingly through the year, perhaps not for the better good of the sport.

The sport's governing body, the FIA, also came under scrutiny, but that was more because its president Max Mosley had been entrapped by a newspaper. Fortunately, the quality of the battle for honours overshadowed that, the intensity building inexorably.

Singapore wasn't the only new round, with another new street race at Valencia having preceded it. This will require some work to make it less industrial. But, of more pressing importance, is that it needs to be changed to introduce some spots for overtaking.

In 2007, Ferrari came from behind to take the drivers' and constructors' titles. In 2008, had its cars not struggled to get heat into their tyres when conditions were either cold or wet, or made mistakes in the pits or had two engine failures, then it would have done the double again.

A prevalence of punctures hurt McLaren, but looking at the speed of the car it was hard to imagine how much its attention must have been dissipated with the Stepneygate dramas of 2007.

BMW Sauber scored its first win, but the ambitious Kubica was correct to scold the team for not matching the development achieved by Ferrari and McLaren. Like Raikkonen, Heidfeld took a while to learn how to get most out of the tyres in qualifying.

Renault looked all at sea and said that it would improve. This it did, with a sudden surge late in the season that saw it vault up the order thanks to Fernando Alonso's two wins. Nelson Piquet Jr was nowhere near the pace in his rookie season.

Toyota also made progress towards the end of the season, taking two podium finishes, but Scuderia Toro Rosso, the team that was once Minardi, beat it to the victory circle when the revelation of the year, Sebastian Vettel, shone in the murk at Monza.

This win hurt its big brother, Red Bull Racing, while Williams was too inconsistent for regular points, Honda gave up and focused on 2009, while Force India brought up the rear when Super Aguri folded after just four grands prix.

AUSTRALIAN GP

Lewis Hamilton put a smile back on the faces at McLaren by giving them a dream start by winning as he pleased. That arch-rivals Ferrari failed to get either of its cars to the finish was cause for even more celebration. BMW Sauber proved to be best of the rest.

McLaren and Lewis Hamilton were desperate to start off with a win and they achieved just that as the 2007 runner-up won with considerable ease.

McLaren wanted to win the opening round more than ever as they felt that a good result would confine their incredibly troubled and expensive 2007 campaign to history.

As ever, the teams only discover their comparative speed when they go out for first practice on the Friday of the opening race of the season. This time, it was immediately clear that Ferrari still had the speed and McLaren looked to be right with them as they put in their first laps in anger around Melbourne's Albert Park circuit, something that many insiders hadn't expected as they felt that McLaren's 2008 challenger would have been compromised by their attention having been divided as they fought the espionage charge against them through the second half of 2007.

It wasn't all about McLaren and Ferrari however, with BMW Sauber contradicting their weak winter testing form to rank first and second in the final practice session before qualifying. Robert Kubica even went on to hold pole position until Hamilton topped it right at the end. The Pole could have gone faster too, but slipped up at Turn 12 and so would start in second place. McLaren newcomer Heikki Kovalainen qualified third fastest, with Felipe Massa fourth for Ferrari, fully 11 places ahead of team-mate Kimi Raikkonen, with the reigning world champion having failed to set a time in the second qualifying session when his F2008's fuel pump failed.

At the start of the race, Hamilton beat Kubica to Turn 1. Kovalainen arrived third, but Massa was desperate to pass and lurched right, damaging his nose on the outside wall at Turn 2. A pit stop would be necessary.

Massa was not the only one pit bound, being followed in by Sebastian Vettel's Toro Rosso and Jenson Button's Honda after a rash of collisions at Turn 1, bringing out the safety car. Giancarlo Fisichella went no further, having had his Force India pitched into a roll by Nelson Piquet Jr, tipping Timo Glock's Toyota into him. Nico Rosberg benefitted the most and guided his Williams from seventh to fourth. Nick Heidfeld ran fifth for BMW Sauber ahead of Toyota's Jarno Trulli.

The complexion of the front group changed as early as lap 16 when Kubica pitted from second, proving that he'd qualified with a light fuel load. This left the McLarens one and two, which is how they ran through to the second round of pit stops. By then, they'd weathered a further safety car period that cost Hamilton a 12.5s lead when Massa tangled with David Coulthard's Red Bull at Turn 1 on lap 25.

The safety car came out for a third time on lap 44 after Glock's Toyota flew over a kerb at Turn 12 and crashed on landing. Luckily for Hamilton, he'd just pitted and was able to resume in the lead, but Heidfeld and Rosberg rose to second and third places at Kovalainen's expense as the Finnish McLaren driver had to wait to make his stop while the pit lane was closed. Having made it as soon as the safety car withdrew, he made it back from eighth to fourth with a lap to go, only to immediately have to cede the place to Fernando Alonso when he hit his pit lane limiter button. Kovalainen ought to have been behind Kubica, too, but the Pole was hit by Kazuki Nakajima's Williams when running behind the safety car.

Sixth place should have gone to Raikkonen - who'd survived two off-track excursions on his advance up the order - but his engine failed with five laps to go, a fate met already by Massa. As there were so few finishers, Raikkonen was credited with a point for eighth, with Toro Rosso debutant Sebastien Bourdais classified seventh despite dropping out of an astonishing fourth place with three laps to go.

MELBOURNE ROUND 01

Date: **16 March 2008** Laps: **58** Distance: **191.110 miles/307.562km**
Weather: **Sunny and hot**

RACE RESULT

Position	Driver	Team	Result	Stops	Qualifying Time	Grid
1	**Lewis Hamilton**	McLaren	1h34m50.616s	2	1m26.714s	1
2	**Nick Heidfeld**	BMW Sauber	1h34m56.094s	2	1m27.236s	5
3	**Nico Rosberg**	Williams	1h34m58.779s	2	1m28.687s	7
4	**Fernando Alonso**	Renault	1h35m07.797s	2	1m26.188s	11
5	**Heikki Kovalainen**	McLaren	1h35m08.630s	2	1m27.079s	3
D*	**Rubens Barrichello**	Honda	1h35m43.069s	3	1m26.173s	10*
6	**Kazuki Nakajima**	Williams	57 laps	3	1m26.413s	13
7	**Sebastien Bourdais**	Toro Rosso	55 laps	2	1m27.446s	17
8	**Kimi Raikkonen**	Ferrari	53 laps/engine	1	no time	15
R	**Robert Kubica**	BMW Sauber	47 laps/collision	2	1m26.869s	2
R	**Timo Glock**	Toyota	43 laps/spun off	1	1m29.593s	19***
R	**Takuma Sato**	Super Aguri	32 laps/transmission	1	1m28.208s	20
R	**Nelson Piquet Jr**	Renault	30 laps/collision	1	1m28.330s	21
R	**Felipe Massa**	Ferrari	29 laps/engine	2	1m27.178s	4
R	**David Coulthard**	Red Bull	25 laps/collision	1	1m29.041s	8
R	**Jarno Trulli**	Toyota	19 laps/battery	0	1m28.527s	6
R	**Adrian Sutil**	Force India	8 laps/hydraulics	0	1m27.859s	18**
R	**Sebastian Vettel**	Toro Rosso	0 laps/collision	0	no time	9
R	**Jenson Button**	Honda	0 laps/collision	0	1m26.259s	12
R	**Mark Webber**	Red Bull	0 laps/collision	0	no time	14
R	**Giancarlo Fisichella**	Force India	0 laps/collision	0	1m27.207s	16
R	**Anthony Davidson**	Super Aguri	0 laps/collision	0	1m29.059s	22

FASTEST LAP: KOVALAINEN, 1M27.418S, 135.704MPH/218.395KPH ON LAP 43
RACE LEADERS: HAMILTON 1-17, 22-42, 47-58; KOVALAINEN 18-21, 43-46
*DISQUALIFIED FOR PITLANE INFRINGEMENT; **STARTED FROM PITLANE; *** FIVE-PLACE GRID PENALTY

TALKING POINT: DID REMOVAL OF TRACTION CONTROL CAUSE THIS?

Driver aids were never popular with the fans. After all, didn't traction control enable inferior drivers to match the better ones as it meant that they had optimum traction and so never spun or got sideways? Turn 1, lap 1 suggested that its banning for 2008 had caught a few out, as cars spun and crashed with abandon. Perhaps the driver who ended up the most embarrassed, his face as red as his Ferrari, was Felipe Massa who simply lost control when he dropped to a lower gear between Turn 1 and Turn 2 in an attempt to outdrag Heikki Kovalainen and lost it, spearing right into the wall. Team-mate Kimi Raikkonen also ran off the circuit twice later in the race...

Hamilton and Kubica show how to do it. Massa markedly does not as his Ferrari spears off track.

MALAYSIAN GP

Ferrari fans must have been delighted that the red cars bounced back from their false start in Australia and 2007 World Champion Kimi Raikkonen won as he pleased in Malaysia. They will have been frustrated by Felipe Massa's patchy form though.

One race, two engine failures and one lucky point was Ferrari's haul from Australia. Two races, one win, 11 points was their tally by the time the teams departed from Sepang a week later and Kimi Raikkonen's sheer speed was enough to convince anyone who watched the Malaysian GP that all was right with the team from Maranello. Well, almost (see panel).

Massa held the advantage as Ferrari locked out the front row of the grid, but there was a surprise behind as third place wasn't filled by a McLaren driver, rather by Jarno Trulli's Toyota ahead of the BMW Saubers of Robert Kubica and Nick Heidfeld then Mark Webber's Red Bull and Fernando Alonso's Renault. This meant

that the best-placed McLaren was Heikki Kovalainen's, in eighth, with Lewis Hamilton ninth. They ought to have been starting higher up, but both were given five-place penalties for running too slowly on their qualifying lap. They were adjudged to have blocked Heidfeld and Alonso respectively, so they were relegated accordingly. The rule would soon be changed to prevent this situation, to stop drivers trying to burn off as little of their fuel load as possible and thus running at speeds low enough for there to be a frightening speed differential with those cars on a flying lap.

Massa led away from Raikkonen, but Trulli wasn't so alert and lost ground into Turn 1 as

he tried to stop Heidfeld from coming past, with Kubica diving into third on his inside. It would get worse for the Italian as he and Heidfeld continued fighting into Turn 2 and both got sideways, allowing Webber to snatch fourth and Hamilton to outdrag him on the run to Turn 4. Heidfeld fell back even further, as Kovalainen, David Coulthard – up from 12th – and Alonso got by.

By dint of having started with one more lap of fuel on board, Raikkonen was able, after trailing Massa through the first stint, to put in a screamer of a lap when the Brazilian pitted and emerge from his own stop in front. Well, in front after the McLarens and then Kubica had

Ferrari's reigning World Champion Kimi Raikkonen lets rip with the champagne after scoring the first victory of his 2008 campaign.

made their pit stops. Raikkonen then waltzed clear, with Massa unable to respond,

Massa struggled on then crashed out on his own. This left Kubica second and, although unable to challenge for the lead, he finished 20s down on Raikkonen and so scored the best result of his career to date.

Kubica was a similar distance ahead of the next finisher, stressing how much McLaren's double grid penalty had neutered the front end of the field, for both McLarens had been able to lap at competitive speed, but their delay by being forced to run behind potentially slower cars hurt them.

It was Kovalainen who claimed the third podium position, becoming the leading McLaren driver when Hamilton lost ground because his right front wheelnut got stuck at his first pit stop, costing him 10s and several positions. Hamilton went on to finish fifth, just behind Trulli, having taken a while to pass Webber who would drop away but still finish in seventh, with Alonso's Renault between he and his Red Bull team-mate Coulthard.

Any hope that Rosberg had that he might make it to the podium for a second race in succession was hampered when he qualified only 16th and then extinguished when he took his Williams's nose off against the back of Timo Glock's Toyota before the end of the opening lap. He eventually made it home a lapped 14th.

SEPANG ROUND 02

Date: **23 March 2008**   Laps: **56** Distance: **192.887 miles/310.407km**
Weather: **Sunny and hot**

RACE RESULT

Position	Driver	Team	Result	Stops	Qualifying Time	Grid
1	**Kimi Raikkonen**	Ferrari	1h31m18.555s	2	1m36.230s	2
2	**Robert Kubica**	BMW Sauber	1h31m38.125s	2	1m36.727s	4
3	**Heikki Kovalainen**	McLaren	1h31m57.005s	2	1m36.613s	8*
4	**Jarno Trulli**	Toyota	1h32m04.387s	2	1m36.711s	3
5	**Lewis Hamilton**	McLaren	1h32m05.103s	2	1m36.709s	9*
6	**Nick Heidfeld**	BMW Sauber	1h32m08.388s	2	1m36.753s	5
7	**Mark Webber**	Red Bull	1h32m26.685s	2	1m37.009s	6
8	**Fernando Alonso**	Renault	1h32m28.596s	2	1m38.450s	7
9	**David Coulthard**	Red Bull	1h32m34.775s	2	1m35.408s	12
10	**Jenson Button**	Honda	1h32m44.769s	2	1m35.208s	11
11	**Nelson Piquet Jr**	Renault	1h32m50.757s	2	1m35.562s	13
12	**Giancarlo Fisichella**	Force India	55 laps	2	1m36.240s	17
13	**Rubens Barrichello**	Honda	55 laps	3	1m35.622s	14
14	**Nico Rosberg**	Williams	55 laps	2	1m35.670s	16
15	**Anthony Davidson**	Super Aguri	55 laps	2	1m37.481s	21
16	**Takuma Sato**	Super Aguri	54 laps	2	1m37.087s	19
17	**Kazuki Nakajima**	Williams	54 laps	2	1m36.388s	22**
R	**Sebastian Vettel**	Toro Rosso	39 laps/engine	1	1m35.648s	15
R	**Felipe Massa**	Ferrari	30 laps/spun off	1	1m35.748s	1
R	**Adrian Sutil**	Force India	5 laps/engine	0	1m37.101s	20
R	**Timo Glock**	Toyota	1 lap/collision	0	1m39.656s	10
R	**Sebastien Bourdais**	Toro Rosso	0 laps/spun off	0	1m36.677s	18

FASTEST LAP: HEIDFELD, 1M35.366S, 130.045MPH/209.288KPH ON LAP 55
RACE LEADERS: MASSA 1-16; RAIKKONEN 17-18, 22-38, 44-56; KUBICA 19-21, 39-43
* 5-PLACE GRID PENALTY FOR BLOCKING ALONSO & HEIDFELD ** 10-PLACE GRID PENALTY FOR CAUSING A COLLISION IN THE AUSTRALIAN GP

TALKING POINT: MASSA FEELS HEAT FOR A SECOND YEAR RUNNING

Felipe Massa doesn't appear to be a driver who can start a season well. For the second year in a row, he was left with little to show after the first two races. And, not surprisingly, the Italian media started to turn on him, suggesting that he'd better shape up or ship out. Qualifying on pole at Sepang will have given him a boost, but Raikkonen had started with more fuel and was ahead after their first stop. In trying to fight back, Massa threw his car off at Turn 8. Coming a year after he had two excursions at Sepang, it did not improve his reputation and he left Sepang knowing that only a win in the next race would get the critics back onside.

Massa hops out of his crashed Ferrari, complete with that sinking feeling that he had to do better.

BAHRAIN GP

For the second year running, it was a race of redemption for Felipe Massa, with victory putting him back in favour at Ferrari. There was nothing that team-mate Kimi Raikkonen could do to beat him. Robert Kubica was again best of the rest.

Kimi Raikkonen flashes past Robert Kubica after the pole-sitting Pole made a mistake and slid wide. Neither could match Felipe Massa's pace, though.

The first task that Felipe Massa had to do on arriving at Bahrain's Sakhir circuit was to prove that he hadn't lost his speed. Being fastest in both Friday practice sessions proved that he hadn't. Remember that he won here in 2007. Second fastest, behind Nico Rosberg, in final practice continued his impressive form.

Then came qualifying, an art that Massa has mastered. But he wasn't smiling when it reached its conclusion. Beating your team-mate is always the first thing that a driver seeks to achieve, and he'd managed that, with a heavier fuel load too. He'd beaten Lewis Hamilton's McLaren, but not the BMW Sauber of Robert Kubica which bagged its first pole.

The gap was 0.027s and everyone was sure that it would have been carrying less fuel, but this wasn't the point for Massa as he'd really wanted pole to put him back on track.

However, Kubica made a terrible start and gifted Massa the lead.

Kubica's start was masterful in comparison to Hamilton's behind him, though, with the Briton having failed to flick a switch early enough and so his anti-stall cut in. Six cars went past him and then he tried too hard to regain places and clattered Fernando Alonso's Renault at Turn 4 and bent his front wing.

Heikki Kovalainen looked to have given McLaren some hope by slotting into third, but

he went wide at Turn 4 and Kimi Raikkonen got the place back.

There was more incident on lap 2, and again Hamilton had a leading role as he tangled with Alonso for a second time. It happened in an unusual place for impact, under acceleration from Turn 3 and it was due to Hamilton's damaged front wing collapsing and allowing his car to be cleaner through the air and ride over the back of the Renault. Hamilton had to pit for repairs, while Alonso lost just one place, to Mark Webber.

At the very same time that this was happening, Kubica hit oil at Turn 4. This had been dropped by Sebastian Vettel's Toro

Rosso as it limped back to the pits to retire after being hit on the opening lap. The Pole slid wide and Raikkonen moved right onto his tail and made a successful move to pass him down the pit straight to give Ferrari first and second in the running order.

Nick Heidfeld, sixth on lap 1, was on the move. He passed Jarno Trulli then hunted down Kovalainen and passed him for fourth into Turn 10 on lap 3, with the Finn suffering severe vibrations after flat-spotting a tyre.

Proving that he had qualified light on fuel, Kubica was first to pit, on lap 17. Raikkonen came in from second on lap 20 and Massa from the lead on lap 21. Importantly, this wasn't to be a day when Raikkonen was able to put in a few blinding laps and emerge in front, so Massa rejoined in the lead and kept it for the rest of the race, save for six laps late on when the BMW Saubers took turns in the lead after long second stints. This didn't help them improve their position though, as they remained third and fourth, with Kubica crossing the line 1.5s behind Raikkonen. This meant that Heidfeld had been bettered again by Kubica and it became apparent that the Pole had bounced back from an indifferent 2007 to become the team's number one.

Kovalainen finished fifth, some way adrift, but not as far off the pace as team-mate Hamilton who ended up a lapped 13th.

BAHRAIN ROUND 03
Date: **6 April 2008** Laps: **57** Distance: **191.530 miles/308.238km**
Weather: **Sunny and hot**

RACE RESULT

Position	Driver	Team	Result	Stops	Qualifying Time	Grid
1	Felipe Massa	Ferrari	1h31m06.970s	2	1m33.123s	2
2	Kimi Raikkonen	Ferrari	1h31m10.309s	2	1m33.418s	4
3	Robert Kubica	BMW Sauber	1h31m11.968s	2	1m33.096s	1
4	Nick Heidfeld	BMW Sauber	1h31m15.379s	2	1m33.737s	6
5	Heikki Kovalainen	McLaren	1h31m33.759s	2	1m33.488s	5
6	Jarno Trulli	Toyota	1h31m48.284s	2	1m33.994s	7
7	Mark Webber	Red Bull	1h31m52.443s	2	1m32.371s	11
8	Nico Rosberg	Williams	1h32m02.859s	2	1m34.015s	8
9	Timo Glock	Toyota	1h32m16.470s	2	1m32.528s	13
10	Fernando Alonso	Renault	1h32m24.151s	2	1m35.115s	10
11	Rubens Barrichello	Honda	1h32m24.832s	2	1m32.508s	12
12	Giancarlo Fisichella	Force India	56 laps	2	1m33.501s	18
13	Lewis Hamilton	McLaren	56 laps	2	1m33.292s	3
14	Kazuki Nakajima	Williams	56 laps	1	1m32.943s	16
15	Sebastien Bourdais	Toro Rosso	56 laps	2	1m32.915s	15
16	Anthony Davidson	Super Aguri	56 laps	2	1m34.140s	21
17	Takuma Sato	Super Aguri	56 laps	2	1m35.725s	22
18	David Coulthard	Red Bull	56 laps	3	1m33.433s	17
19	Adrian Sutil	Force India	55 laps	3	1m33.845s	20
R	Nelson Piquet Jr	Renault	40 laps/gearbox	2	1m32.790s	14
R	Jenson Button	Honda	19 laps/collision	2	1m35.057s	9
R	Sebastian Vettel	Toro Rosso	0 laps/collision	0	1m33.562s	19

FASTEST LAP: KOVALAINEN, 1M33.193S, 129.905MPH/209.062KPH ON LAP 49
RACE LEADERS: MASSA 1-39, 46-57; KUBICA 40-41; HEIDFELD 42-45

TALKING POINT: FIA CHIEF IN SPOTLIGHT AFTER NEWSPAPER SCOOP

Max Mosley was under scrutiny like never before, as tabloid *The News of the World* had run a photo showing the FIA President with five prostitutes. He had apologised to FIA members, stating that it was something that had happened in private and that the exposé didn't prevent him from doing his job. His defiance wasn't convincing, as he didn't attend the Bahrain GP. Indeed, the crown prince had asked him not to. The matter of whether he should remain as President was to be put to the general assembly in June and he duly won that, but the manufacturers said that they were less than happy and talk of a breakaway championship was mooted.

FIA President Max Mosley was defiant, but stayed away from the paddock until the Monaco GP.

SPANISH GP

Roundly beaten in Bahrain, Kimi Raikkonen was back on top form in Barcelona, reversing the order as he kept Felipe Massa behind him. Lewis Hamilton had a better run, but the race will be remembered by many for Heikki Kovalainen's crash.

No one could live with the pace of the Ferraris at the Circuit de Catalunya and Kimi Raikkonen raced to victory ahead of his team-mate Felipe Massa.

Pole position, check. Lead all the way, check. Set fastest lap, check. Job done, check. And, with that list complete, Kimi Raikkonen was able to leave Spain in better mood than he had left the previous race in the Middle East.

The race was not a classic and, as is often the case at the Circuit de Catalunya, there was next to no overtaking. But, after starting from pole and winning the drag to Turn 1, this concerned Raikkonen not one jot.

To the surprise of many, Fernando Alonso qualified second. Everyone said that he had qualified with a light fuel load, just to put on a show for his home fans. That proved to be the case when he was the first to pit, some five

laps earlier than most of his rivals. However, his hopes of taking the lead came to naught as he struggled to find grip for his getaway from the dirty side of the grid, and Massa slotted into second.

Raikkonen's initial advantage was reined in as the safety car came out in his path as he started the second lap, as an accident between Adrian Sutil, who messed up a pass on David Coulthard at Turn 4, and Sebastian Vettel left debris on the track.

Raikkonen streaked away when the safety car withdrew, with Massa second and Alonso trailed by Hamilton, Kubica and Kovalainen.

The safety car came out again on lap 23

because of a frightening accident that befell Kovalainen. He had been on his in-lap when a wheel rim failed and deflated his left front tyre just as he crested the hill at Turn 9 at 145mph, leaving him with no steering. He ploughed across the gravel into the tyre wall. In fact, he ended up buried beneath it. There was considerable concern, but his car had stayed intact and he emerged bruised but safe.

The safety car didn't affect the leading drivers, as they'd pitted, but it wrecked Nick Heidfeld's race, as he had been running with a heavy fuel load and all hopes of taking a pitch at the McLarens were snuffed out. With his tank all but dry, he had to pit under the safety car and accept the stop-go penalty this brings. It dropped him to the tail.

Raikkonen pulled away at ease for a second time and led all the way to the finish, with Massa unable to get close enough to score his second win from four starts and extend his championship lead to nine points over Hamilton who finished third.

Kubica claimed fourth, but there was then a half-minute void before Mark Webber came home fifth. Jenson Button was next, scoring his first points of the year for Honda. He'd started 13th and driven a strong race, but was fortunate to escape banging wheels in the pits when Giancarlo Fisichella pulled out from his stop. The Italian had already clashed with the other Honda on the way in. This took off Barrichello's front wing and ended what could also have been a point-scoring race. Nico Rosberg was another to retire, his engine failing when he was seventh.

So, the final points went to Kazuki Nakajima and Jarno Trulli, the Italian having lost a couple of places when he was called in to have his front wing replaced, only for the team to realise that it was team-mate Timo Glock's wing that had been damaged and so waving Trulli through.

Any hope of glory for the home fans disappeared when Alonso retired from fifth place when his Renault's engine failed.

BARCELONA ROUND 04

Date: **27 April 2008** Laps: **66** Distance: **190.825 miles/307.104km**
Weather: **Sunny and dry**

RACE RESULT

Position	Driver	Team	Result	Stops	Qualifying Time	Grid
1	Kimi Raikkonen	Ferrari	1h38m19.051s	2	1m21.813s	1
2	Felipe Massa	Ferrari	1h38m22.279s	2	1m22.058s	3
3	Lewis Hamilton	McLaren	1h38m23.238s	2	1m22.096s	5
4	Robert Kubica	BMW Sauber	1h38m24.745s	2	1m22.065s	4
5	Mark Webber	Red Bull	1h38m54.989s	2	1m22.429s	7
6	Jenson Button	Honda	1h39m12.061s	2	1m21.211s	13
7	Kazuki Nakajima	Williams	1h39m17.295s	2	1m21.117s	12
8	Jarno Trulli	Toyota	1h39m18.486s	2	1m22.529s	8
9	Nick Heidfeld	BMW Sauber	1h39m22.124s	3	1m22.542s	9
10	Giancarlo Fisichella	Force India	65 laps	2	1m22.516s	19
11	Timo Glock	Toyota	65 laps	3	1m21.230s	14
12	David Coulthard	Red Bull	65 laps	3	1m21.810s	17
13	Takuma Sato	Super Aguri	65 laps	2	1m23.496s	22
R	Nico Rosberg	Williams	41 laps/engine	1	1m21.349s	15
R	Fernando Alonso	Renault	34 laps/engine	1	1m21.904s	2
R	Rubens Barrichello	Honda	34 laps/crash damage	2	1m21.049s	11
R	Heikki Kovalainen	McLaren	21 laps/spun off	0	1m22.231s	6
R	Anthony Davidson	Super Aguri	8 laps/radiator	0	1m23.318s	21
R	Sebastien Bourdais	Toro Rosso	7 laps/crash damage	0	1m21.724s	16
R	Nelson Piquet Jr	Renault	6 laps/accident	0	1m22.699s	10
R	Sebastian Vettel	Toro Rosso	0 laps/accident	0	1m22.108s	18
R	Adrian Sutil	Force India	0 laps/accident	0	1m23.224s	20

FASTEST LAP: RAIKKONEN, 1M21.670S, 127.500MPH/205.192KPH ON LAP 46
RACE LEADERS: RAIKKONEN 1-20, 25-66; HAMILTON 21; HEIDFELD 22-24

TALKING POINT: TEAMS DISCUSS HOW TO IMPROVE THE SHOW

It was fitting that the teams sat down at the Spanish GP to discuss how to make the racing more exciting. For the circuit is one that allows precious little overtaking. The teams discussed how the rules might be amended to improve the show. Cutting downforce was discussed and one of the suggestions for 2009 was to fit the cars with adjustable front wing flaps so that drivers could flip them up when running behind another car, where they need to be to be close enough to pass. The Overtaking Group pushed for a simpler aero package with limited rear diffusers to tidy the airflow behind each car, thus also making it less turbulent for the chasing car.

The Ferraris lead Alonso et al, but this train of cars at Barcelona was unable to produce overtaking.

TURKISH GP

Felipe Massa loves the Turkish GP, but that's not surprising as he notched up his third straight win there to put himself back in the championship reckoning. Lewis Hamilton likes it too, as his masterful three-stop strategy was rewarded with second position.

Felipe Massa smiles as befits a winner, Lewis Hamilton smiles as someone relieved to have landed a result, and Kimi Raikkonen grimaces and bears it.

There were two brilliant drives at Istanbul Park, by Felipe Massa and Lewis Hamilton. They went about their jobs in very different ways, but the fact that the McLaren driver described his run to second as his best race ever suggested that he knew just how hard he had had to push to make his three-stop strategy work against the Ferraris.

The Ferrari had the edge on tyre preservation in Turkey, as the McLarens were as fast but Hamilton's wore out its right front tyre in fewer laps. Thus the need for the three-stop run and a tactical aggression from McLaren that was not unlike that shown by their arch-rivals in Hungary in 1998 when Michael Schumacher ran a three-

stop strategy as the only way to match the McLarens, driving each race lap as though it was a qualifying flier. And it worked.

Hamilton was unable to prevent the pole star of the early part of the season, Massa, from being on top in qualifying again. Heikki Kovalainen was second fastest, just 0.191s behind Massa and 0.115s ahead of Hamilton, with Kimi Raikkonen a further blink of an eye behind. Kovalainen's performance deserved considerable praise as, not only was he making his first appearance since his heavy shunt in the Spanish GP, but he was carrying a heavier fuel load than Massa by as much as four laps. So, it looked as though the race was going to be a classic.

Massa led away, but Kovalainen's day turned sharply downhill when Raikkonen clipped his left rear at Turn 1, sending the Finn pitwards with a puncture.

This wasn't the only contact on the opening lap, either, as Giancarlo Fisichella hit the rear of Kazuki Nakajima's Williams and the Force India rose high into the air before smashing down into retirement.

Raikkonen was slightly delayed by his clash with Kovalainen and ended the first lap in fifth, behind Robert Kubica who had passed him on the blast off the grid and then by a fast-starting Fernando Alonso. Once more, though, Alonso's Renault had run light on fuel in qualifying to ensure a good grid position and was the first to make a pit stop, on lap 15.

Hamilton came in a lap later, frustrated at not having been able to get ahead of Massa at the start so that he could attempt to build a margin that would cancel out the time lost by his planned extra pit visit. He was pleased that the duo had left the rest of the field in their wake, as Kubica wasn't able to match their pace. Hamilton emerged in sixth place, but was second again once the frontrunners had called in for the first of their two planned pit stops, with Raikkonen having got past Kubica for third.

Massa was leading again, but Hamilton knew that he had to overtake him if he was to stand any chance of winning. And this he did down the inside on lap 24 with a brilliant move. He then pulled away at a second per lap, but was third behind Massa and Raikkonen when he emerged from his second stop on lap 32. He would rise to second again after his final stop, but Massa was just too good on the day.

So, when the dust settled, with Massa beaming, Hamilton pleased with himself and Raikkonen typically taciturn, poor Kovalainen was left to rue the scuppering of a race that could well have resulted in his maiden grand prix win. He'd had the speed, but not the fortune.

ISTANBUL PARK ROUND 05

Date: **11 May 2008** Laps: **58** Distance: **192.388 miles/309.619km**
Weather: **Sunny and warm**

RACE RESULT

Position	Driver	Team	Result	Stops	Qualifying Time	Grid
1	Felipe Massa	Ferrari	1h26m49.451s	2	1m27.617s	1
2	Lewis Hamilton	McLaren	1h26m53.230s	3	1m27.923s	3
3	Kimi Raikkonen	Ferrari	1h26m53.722s	2	1m27.936s	4
4	Robert Kubica	BMW Sauber	1h27m11.396s	2	1m28.390s	5
5	Nick Heidfeld	BMW Sauber	1h27m28.192s	2	1m28.882s	9
6	Fernando Alonso	Renault	1h27m43.175s	2	1m28.422s	7
7	Mark Webber	Red Bull	1h27m53.680s	2	1mx28.417s	6
8	Nico Rosberg	Williams	1h28m00.857s	2	1m27.012s	11
9	David Coulthard	Red Bull	1h28m04.721s	2	1m29.959s	10
10	Jarno Trulli	Toyota	1h28m05.795s	2	1m28.836s	8
11	Jenson Button	Honda	57 laps	1	1m27.298s	13
12	Heikki Kovalainen	McLaren	57 laps	3	1m27.808s	2
13	Timo Glock	Toyota	57 laps	1	1m27.806s	15
14	Rubens Barrichello	Honda	57 laps	1	1m27.219s	12
15	Nelson Piquet Jr	Renault	57 laps	2	1m27.568s	17
16	Adrian Sutil	Force India	57 laps	3	1m28.325s	19
17	Sebastian Vettel	Toro Rosso	57 laps	4	1m27.412s	14
R	Sebastien Bourdais	Toro Rosso	24 laps/spun off	1	1m27.621s	18
R	Kazuki Nakajima	Williams	1 lap/collision	0	1m27.547s	16
R	Giancarlo Fisichella	Force India	0 laps/collision	0	1m27.807s	20*

FASTEST LAP: RAIKKONEN, 1M26.506S, 138.034MPH/222.145KPH ON LAP 20
RACE LEADERS: MASSA 1-19, 22-23, 33-40, 46-58; RAIKKONEN 20-21, 41-43; HAMILTON 24-32, 44-45
* 3-PLACE GRID PENALTY FOR PASSING RED LIGHT AT PIT EXIT

TALKING POINT: BARRICHELLO BECOMES MOST EXPERIENCED DRIVER

Rubens Barrichello broke Riccardo Patrese's record for grand prix starts when he contested his 257th grand prix in Turkey. He would have loved to have scored even a point, his first of the year, but the Honda racer ended up a lapped 14th. This is not where you would have expected a driver of his calibre to be finishing. Don't forget this was the driver who ran in third place in wet/dry conditions for Jordan at Donington Park in 1993 in only his third start and went on to win nine grands prix with Ferrari. However, his move to Honda has yet to look likely to add to that tally. His RA108 may not have been quick, but at least it carried a special livery for the occasion.

The pit board says it all for Honda racer Barrichello: 257 grands prix and still going strong.

MONACO GP

Rain, punctures and hitting barriers were all part of the mix, but Lewis Hamilton was able to score the win that he wanted more than any other. With Kimi Raikkonen out of the points, it put the Briton into the championship lead too.

With a Ferrari lock-out of the front row, it was likely that either pole-sitter Felipe Massa or Kimi Raikkonen would end the day victorious. But rain fell before the start and was sure to make the early laps something of a lottery.

Anxious not to lose ground in their spray, Lewis Hamilton dived past Raikkonen into second before they reached Ste Devote. His next target was Massa, but seeing through his spray was tricky. All behind him were faced with a similar problem, the field stringing out in a way that it never would in the dry.

Because of this, Hamilton didn't lose too much time when he had to make an unplanned pit stop on lap 6, coming out in fifth. Why had he stopped? Because he'd run wide and hit the barrier at Tabac. The damage was only a punctured right rear and a rapid radio call enabled the pit crew to be ready in time with a replacement. But, what really saved him was the fact that the safety car was deployed immediately afterwards and, refuelled with a heavy load, he was able to make up ground as the field bunched, wiping out most of his 30s deficit to Massa. He got back to fourth when Fernando Alonso pitted as he'd punctured a tyre against the barriers as well.

The reason that the safety car had had to be deployed was David Coulthard had crashed at Massenet and Sebastien Bourdais spun when he arrived on the scene.

Hamilton's fourth became third on lap 13 when Raikkonen came in for a drive-through penalty for not having had his tyres fitted before the three-minute board on the grid.

On the very same lap, Alonso made a dive to pass Nick Heidfeld for fifth at the hairpin and spun the German sideways.

Massa came under pressure from Robert Kubica, and slipped up under braking for Ste Devote on lap 16, letting the BMW Sauber into the lead. The Pole would stay in front until he pitted on lap 26, allowing Hamilton to reach second. Seven laps later, Hamilton hit the front when Massa came in.

Lewis Hamilton was in scintillating form on the streets of Monaco and raced to victory despite puncturing a tyre against the barriers early in the race.

From there, lapping with ease, Hamilton went on and on until lap 54, running an incredibly long second stint, before pitting for the final time. Massa had no answer to the McLaren driver's pace and then lost second place to Kubica when he made his final stop.

Hamilton's second scare came on lap 60 when he reached Piscine and was confronted by debris where Nico Rosberg had dropped his Williams. It brought out the safety car but he stayed in front when it withdrew.

Amazingly Adrian Sutil had been heading for fourth for Force India, but he had the recovering Raikkonen on his tail and was tipped out of the race, allowing Mark Webber to take his fifth consecutive points finish.

Behind him, Sebastian Vettel rose from 19th to fifth, making particular progress as the track dried. But for losing his front wing after an aggressive first lap, Jenson Button could have helped Honda to a double helping of points. As it was, just Rubens Barrichello scored, finishing sixth, with Kazuki Nakajima seventh and Heikki Kovalainen eighth.

The Finn's hopes of nailing a good result after his disappointments in Spain and Turkey were dealt a blow before the start as an electrical fault left him unable to change gear and so he had to start from the pit lane.

Nelson Piquet Jr continued his torrid run with another crash, when running 15th.

MONACO ROUND 06

Date: **25 May 2008** Laps: **76** Distance: **157.700 miles/253.794km**
Weather: **Raining then damp**

RACE RESULT

Position	Driver	Team	Result	Stops	Qualifying Time	Grid
1	Lewis Hamilton	McLaren	2h00m42.742s	2	1m15.839s	3
2	Robert Kubica	BMW Sauber	2h00m45.806s	2	1m16.171s	5
3	Felipe Massa	Ferrari	2h00m47.553s	2	1m15.787s	1
4	Mark Webber	Red Bull	2h01m02.037s	1	1m17.343s	9
5	Sebastian Vettel	Toro Rosso	2h01m07.399s	1	1m16.955s	19*
6	Rubens Barrichello	Honda	2h01m11.150s	1	1m16.537s	14
7	Kazuki Nakajima	Williams	2h01m12.922s	1	1m16.479s	13
8	Heikki Kovalainen	McLaren	2h01m15.933s	2	1m16.165s	4
9	Kimi Raikkonen	Ferrari	2h01m16.534s	4	1m15.815s	2
10	Fernando Alonso	Renault	75 laps	3	1m16.852s	7
11	Jenson Button	Honda	75 laps	3	1m16.101s	11
12	Timo Glock	Toyota	75 laps	3	1m15.907s	10
13	Jarno Trulli	Toyota	75 laps	3	1m17.203s	8
14	Nick Heidfeld	BMW Sauber	72 laps	3	1m16.455s	12
R	Adrian Sutil	Force India	67 laps/collision	1	1m17.225s	18
R	Nico Rosberg	Williams	59 laps/spun off	4	1m16.548s	6
R	Nelson Piquet Jr	Renault	47 laps/spun off	1	1m16.933s	17
R	Giancarlo Fisichella	Force India	36 laps/gearbox	0	1m17.823s	20*
R	David Coulthard	Red Bull	7 laps/spun off	0	No time	15*
R	Sebastien Bourdais	Toro Rosso	7 laps/collision	0	1m16.806s	16

FASTEST LAP: RAIKKONEN, 1M16.689S, 97.424MPH/156.789KPH ON LAP 74
RACE LEADERS: MASSA 1-15, 26-32; KUBICA 16-25; HAMILTON 33-76
* 5-PLACE PENALTY FOR CHANGING GEARBOX

TALKING POINT: SUTIL'S DREAM DRIVE FOR FORCE INDIA FALLS SHORT

Sport can be cruel, and those who follow it are inured to it, but there was universal sympathy for the way in which Adrian Sutil's race was brought to a close. He had started his unfancied Force India 18th. With the inevitable accidents factored in, it was thought that it would take at least 10 retirements to help him towards points, as overtaking is so hard on this narrow circuit. Yet, he leapt to 12th on lap 1 and kept his cool as others stumbled. By the second of his pit stops, he was fourth, heading for his first points. Then, with nine laps to go, Kimi Raikkonen lost control behind him and knocked his car into retirement. It was reckoned that this cost his team £5m.

The loss of points for Adrian Sutil could have cost Force India as much as £5m in lost revenue.

CANADIAN GP

This is a race that will be remembered for two things. Firstly, for Robert Kubica and BMW Sauber securing their first win. Secondly, for a split-second incident tipping Lewis Hamilton's season off the rails just as he looked set for victory.

One pit stop, two broken cars. This is the aftermath of race leader Lewis Hamilton failing to notice a red light at pit exit, hitting Raikkonen's Ferrari.

Few Canadian GPs have run smoothly since the race moved to Montreal in the 1970s. If anything, the races on the Circuit Gilles Villeneuve have become more topsy-turvy, and this was up there with the wild ones.

Buoyed by his somewhat fortunate victory at Monaco and by returning to the scene of his maiden win, Lewis Hamilton was in scorching form, his pole lap 0.612s faster than second-placed Robert Kubica, but an incident that brought out the safety car has masked forever just how much or how little fuel his McLaren had been carrying.

Hamilton was dominant up to this point, with Kubica holding an increasingly distant second from Kimi Raikkonen, with Nico Rosberg fourth, Fernando Alonso fifth and Felipe Massa sixth. There had already been

drivers sliding wide as the track surface broke up, but it took Adrian Sutil parking his broken down Force India at the side of the track at Turn 3 to bring out the safety car.

The drivers, all aware that their first pit stops were approaching, were anxious to pit and were able to do so on lap 19 when the pit lane was opened again. Two-thirds of the drivers came in together, nose-to-tail behind Hamilton, but Kubica and Raikkonen were turned around more swiftly.

They drove, limiters activated, towards the exit, but stopped as the red light was on, a novelty caused at Montreal by the lengthy loop before the point at which the pit exit road rejoins it at Turn 2. Hamilton failed to heed the red light and slammed into the back of Raikkonen, just missing Kubica. In

turn, Rosberg slid into Hamilton's McLaren. Hamilton and Rosberg, who was able to continue, were both later slapped with a 10-place grid penalty for the following race.

Thanking his lucky stars, Kubica's car was unscathed and rejoined the race, in 10th, but he was still to have a role to play.

The list of race leaders was greater than it had been for years as several drivers had decided not to pit, having qualified with a heavy fuel load with the intention of stopping just once. One of these was Nick Heidfeld, who led for 10 laps before pitting, blazing away at the front as he tried to pull out as much of a gap as possible. And this was to become the story of the remainder of the race as team-mate Kubica was still 10th, held up by Sebastian Vettel.

Heidfeld stayed out one lap longer than his team wanted him to, in an attempt to eke out another fraction of a second over his team-mate. He emerged from his stop just ahead of Kubica. He was heavier, though, and tried all he could to stay ahead, but he couldn't hold out and Kubica was by on lap 31, albeit only moving into seventh place.

Rubens Barrichello, David Coulthard, Jarno Trulli and Timo Glock took turns in the lead before their stops. When they had made them, it was Kubica in the lead, sprinting for all he was worth now that he was no longer delayed by one-stopping cars, with Heidfeld second and Alonso third until the Spaniard crashed when trying to find a way past.

Kubica then made Poland proud by opening out enough of a gap to make his second stop and emerge in a lead he was to keep to the finish. Not only was this his first win, but it put him into the points lead.

Coulthard showed how he can keep his cool when others around him are losing theirs to not only score the first points of his campaign but to return to the podium for the first time since Monaco 2006.

Glock held off Massa for fourth, with the Ferrari driver having lost ground when his fuel rig failed in the massed scramble to the pits behind the safety car and he was required to pit again next time around.

MONTREAL ROUND 07

Date: **8 June 2008** Laps: **70** Distance: **189.686 miles/305.270km**
Weather: **Sunny and hot**

RACE RESULT

Position	Driver	Team	Result	Stops	Qualifying Time	Grid
1	**Robert Kubica**	BMW Sauber	1h36m24.447s	2	1m18.498s	2
2	**Nick Heidfeld**	BMW Sauber	1h36m40.942s	1	1m19.633s	8
3	**David Coulthard**	Red Bull	1h36m47.799s	1	1m18.238s	13
4	**Timo Glock**	Toyota	1h37m07.074s	1	1m18.031s	11
5	**Felipe Massa**	Ferrari	1h37m08.381s	3	1m19.048s	6
6	**Jarno Trulli**	Toyota	1h37m12.222s	1	1m18.327s	14
7	**Rubens Barrichello**	Honda	1h37m18.044s	1	1m20.848s	9
8	**Sebastian Vettel**	Toro Rosso	1h37m18.567s	1	no time	18^
9	**Heikki Kovalainen**	McLaren	1h37m18.880s	2	1m19.089s	7
10	**Nico Rosberg**	Williams	1h37m22.196s	3	1m18.844s	5
11	**Jenson Button**	Honda	1h37m31.987s	3	1m23.565s	20*^
12	**Mark Webber**	Red Bull	1h37m35.676s	2	no time	10
13	**Sebastien Bourdais**	Toro Rosso	69 laps	2	1m18.916s	19*
R	**Giancarlo Fisichella**	Force India	51 laps/spun off	2	1m19.165s	17
R	**Kazuki Nakajima**	Williams	46 laps/collision	1	1m18.062s	12
R	**Fernando Alonso**	Renault	44 laps/spun off	1	1m18.746s	4
R	**Nelson Piquet Jr**	Renault	39 laps/brakes	1	1m18.393s	15
R	**Kimi Raikkonen**	Ferrari	19 laps/collision	1	1m18.735s	3
R	**Lewis Hamilton**	McLaren	19 laps/collision	1	1m17.886s	1
R	**Adrian Sutil**	Force India	13 laps/gearbox	0	1m19.108s	16

FASTEST LAP: KOVALAINEN, 1M17.387S, 126.058MPH/202.871KPH ON LAP 14
RACE LEADERS: HAMILTON 1-18; HEIDFELD 19-28; BARRICHELLO 29-35; COULTHARD 36; TRULLI 37-38; GLOCK 39-41; KUBICA 42-70
* 5-PLACE PENALTY FOR CHANGING GEARBOX. ^ STARTED FROM THE PIT LANE

TALKING POINT: BMW SAUBER BREAKS INTO THE BIG TIME

BMW had had a shot at Formula 1 in the 1960s, but with F2 machinery. Building engines for Brabham, Benetton and Arrows was their next involvement in the 1980s before they tried again with Williams in 2000, becoming winners through Ralf Schumacher. Conversely, Sauber had come to F1 in 1993, from sports car racing. Short on finance, the team failed to advance beyond the midfield, even when buoyed with cash from Malaysian oil company Petronas. When BMW and Williams split, BMW motorsport chief Mario Theissen threw BMW's money and engineering expertise at a partnership with Sauber for 2006 and this landmark 1-2 was their reward.

Mario Theissen and Willy Rampf join the drivers in celebrating BMW Sauber's inaugural victory.

FRENCH GP

Ferrari were back on top in France, racing to a one-two, but the order was reversed when a broken exhaust slowed Kimi Raikkonen and Felipe Massa raced through for the third win of his 2008 campaign, with Jarno Trulli coming home third for Toyota.

Lewis Hamilton arrived at Magny-Cours knowing that not only had he blown a potential win in the previous race in Canada by crashing into Kimi Raikkonen at pit exit, but that he would be put back 10 positions on the grid - as would Nico Rosberg's Williams - for his troubles. Only pole position would do in Hamilton's attempt to minimise the damage, but he ended up third behind the Ferrari duo, and so would start down in 13th.

Unlucky 13 it proved to be, as he was adjudged to have offended on his flying first lap when he gained three places in passing Nick Heidfeld, Sebastian Vettel and the slow-starting David Coulthard. The problem came when he passed Vettel's Toro Rosso into the downhill Nurburgring chicane, but failed to make the exit of the corner without running off the track. He decided that he hadn't gained an advantage from this. But, infuriatingly and expensively for Hamilton and McLaren, the stewards decided that he had and requested that he call to the pits for a drivethrough penalty, thus removing any chance of scoring points and potentially making a major dent in his title challenge.

Raikkonen had led away, with Massa tucking into second place as Fernando Alonso tried to hold onto third place. But, even though he had qualified with a light fuel load, he was beaten away by Trulli and Robert Kubica, with the Red Bulls being passed left-and-right as they too struggled for traction. The Spaniard battled past the Pole at the hairpin, but there was nothing he could do about the Italian.

This was how the order remained at the front until Alonso brought his Renault in for a pit stop as early as lap 15, elevating Timo Glock to fifth in the second Toyota.

Massa stayed out longest of this group, but resumed second behind Raikkonen and looked set to stay there until he started to close at half-distance. It soon became apparent that the Finn was slowing and it turned out that one of his exhaust tail pipes had come loose, costing him power. Massa closed in and moved ahead on lap 39. The race, from there was all his, even withstanding a rain shower late in the race, as Raikkonen fell back towards Trulli's third-placed Toyota, his 30s cushion being whittled away with every lap. Yet, the race reached its conclusion with Trulli still 10s behind, nevertheless delighted with his first podium finish since 2005.

It was Ferrari all the way in France, but the advantage only swung Felipe Massa's way when Kimi Raikkonen's car was slowed by a broken exhaust.

One might have thought that Heikki Kovalainen ought to be able to challenge at Magny-Cours, but he had been put back five places on the grid for obstructing Mark Webber in qualifying, dropping him to 10th. He rose to seventh after making his first pit stop late, then got past Alonso – who had been changed from a three-stop strategy to a two-stopper after failing to keep Trulli behind him at the start – and Kubica. By the end, he was right on Trulli's tail, even alongside on the last lap but one, but unable to get by for third.

Kubica ended up fifth, with Webber back in the points in sixth place, heading home a driver who simply had to deliver to keep his seat. This was Nelson Piquet Jr and his first points were timely. That team-mate Alonso finished behind him, in eighth, was further validation of Nelsinho's progress.

Bemoaning the fact that he had lost four positions before the first corner on the opening lap, falling to 11th, David Coulthard ended up ninth, just out of the points for the third time in eight races.

Hamilton rounded out the top-10, and he truly must have understood the phrase "double whammy", as the ramifications of his loss of attention as he accelerated away from his pit stop in Canada proved to be twice as bad as the loss of 10 likely championship points in Montreal.

MAGNY-COURS ROUND 08

Date:**22 June 2008** Laps: **70** Distance: **191.870 miles/308.785km**
Weather: **Damp, then rain at end**

RACE RESULT

Position	Driver	Team	Result	Stops	Qualifying Time	Grid
1	**Felipe Massa**	Ferrari	1h31m50.245s	2	1m16.490s	2
2	**Kimi Raikkonen**	Ferrari	1h32m08.229s	2	1m16.449s	1
3	**Jarno Trulli**	Toyota	1h32m18.495s	2	1m16.920s	4
4	**Heikki Kovalainen**	McLaren	1h32m19.174s	2	1m16.944s	10*
5	**Robert Kubica**	BMW Sauber	1h32m20.757s	2	1m17.037s	5
6	**Mark Webber**	Red Bull	1h32m30.549s	2	1m17.233s	6
7	**Nelson Piquet Jr**	Renault	1h32m31.278s	2	1m15.770s	9
8	**Fernando Alonso**	Renault	1h32m33.617s	2	1m16.840s	3
9	**David Coulthard**	Red Bull	1h32m41.317s	2	1m17.426s	7
10	**Lewis Hamilton**	McLaren	1h32m44.766s	3	1m16.693s	13**
11	**Timo Glock**	Toyota	1h32m47.983s	2	1m17.596s	8
12	**Sebastian Vettel**	Toro Rosso	1h32m48.310s	2	1m15.816s	12
13	**Nick Heidfeld**	BMW Sauber	1h32m52.324s	2	1m15.786s	11
14	**Rubens Barrichello**	Honda	69 laps	2	1m16.330s	20***
15	**Kazuki Nakajima**	Williams	69 laps	2	1m16.243s	15
16	**Nico Rosberg**	Williams	69 laps	1	1m16.235s	19**
17	**Sebastien Bourdais**	Toro Rosso	69 laps	2	1m16.045s	14
18	**Giancarlo Fisichella**	Force India	69 laps	2	1m16.971s	17
19	**Adrian Sutil**	Force India	69 laps	2	1m17.053s	18
R	**Jenson Button**	Honda	16 laps/collision damage	1	1m16.306s	16

FASTEST LAP: RAIKKONEN, 1M16.630S, 128.763MPH/207.224KPH ON LAP 16
RACE LEADERS: RAIKKONEN 1-21, 24-38; MASSA 22-23, 39-70
* 5-PLACE PENALTY FOR OBSTRUCTION IN QUALIFYING. ** 10-PLACE PENALTY FOR PIT LANE ACCIDENT IN CANADA. *** 5-PLACE PENALTY FOR GEARBOX CHANGE

TALKING POINT: TOYOTA PAYS TRIBUTE TO OVE ANDERSSON

The loss of Ove Andersson, former boss of Toyota Motorsport, in an accident in a historic rally in South Africa came as a shock. He hadn't spent many years in the paddock, after decades in rallying, but the big Swede's affable nature made him instantly popular, which explained why people from all the teams took the time to sign a book of condolence. So, it was with great sadness that Toyota headed to the French GP and it was seen as a fitting tribute that Toyota's upturn in form and Jarno Trulli's feisty drive resulted in Toyota's first podium since Ralf Schumacher came third in Australia in 2006. The cars ran with a black band across their noses in Ove's memory.

Jarno Trulli had extra reason to smile when Toyota's upturn in form helped him to third place.

BRITISH GP

Battered by the press for his two non-scores, Lewis Hamilton fought back in the best way, by winning at Silverstone. This was more than just winning, though, as he delivered a classic wet weather drive in treacherous and ever-changing conditions.

McLaren chief operating officer Martin Whitmarsh tries to keep out of the way as Heidfeld, Hamilton and Barrichello spray the bubbly on the podium.

There had been menace in the air in the run-up to the British GP, as the ever fickle British press had turned on Lewis Hamilton. Build them up and knock them down had long been the way of the country's media and Lewis had provided them with ammunition by his unnecessarily nonchalant dismissal of his potentially season-wrecking faux pas at the Canadian GP, then backed it up with failing to score in the French GP.

Strong form through practice put this to the backburner. Especially when the press noticed the esteem in which Hamilton was held by the fans thronging the spectator banking. So, when he showed a strong hand in the early stages of qualifying, hopes were high. Three-quarters of the way around his flying lap in the third qualifying session,

he was set to lower the standard by 0.75s, but then he ran wide. There was time for one more roll of the dice, but Hamilton was cautious and ended up fourth. To throw matters into confusion, pole position went for the first time to his team-mate Heikki Kovalainen. Of course, this asked questions about what fuel load Kovalainen had been carrying, but Hamilton appeared to be confident, so the inference was perhaps that the Finn had been running light.

This didn't prove to be the case, but rain before the start masked much of this. Kovalainen led away and Hamilton made an exceptional start to slot into second place by Copse. Indeed, he came within a whisker of taking the lead of his home race.

Behind them, Mark Webber, who had

started from Red Bull Racing's first ever front row grid position, spun at Becketts when he tried to repass Kimi Raikkonen.

Red Bull Racing's woes didn't end there, as David Coulthard, who had announced that this would be his final British GP, had a run on Sebastian Vettel who had lost momentum out of Abbey and dived down his inside into Priory, only to find the gap closing, taking both off.

Hamilton hunted down Kovalainen and took the lead at Stowe on lap 5. The crowd went wild. Then, despite having a visor that kept fogging up on one side, Hamilton pulled away as his team-mate struggled with rear tyre wear problems. Kovalainen spun at Abbey and Raikkonen moved into second place. Then, as the track began to dry, he started to close in on Hamilton.

When they both pitted on lap 21, they were almost together, but Hamilton just stayed ahead. What had happened in the Ferrari pit stop, though, was to shape the race, for Raikkonen had been left on the same set of intermediate tyres. Hamiton was on a new set. And, as they got up to speed, the rain fell again and Raikkonen dropped back by as many as half a dozen seconds per lap. So, it wasn't yet half distance, but the race was run. It was Hamilton's.

Kovalainen caught Raikkonen and dived into second at Luffield, only to run wide and let Nick Heidfeld take his BMW Sauber past both. Then the rain intensified on lap 35 and cars were spinning off or running wide everywhere. Rubens Barrichello called in for extreme wet tyres and transformed himself from a midfield runner into the fastest driver on the track. Jenson Button followed suit. Hamilton pitted, but had such a lead that he elected to go out on another set of intermediate tyres.

Barrichello's charge took him to second place, unable to get close to Hamilton, but a final pit stop dropped him behind Heidfeld, although he was delighted with his first podium finish since 2005. Button ought to have finished well, too, but he slid off and Robert Kubica followed suit.

SILVERSTONE ROUND 09

Date: **6 July 2008** Laps: **60** Distance: **191.640 miles/308.415km**
Weather: **Rain**

RACE RESULT

Position	Driver	Team	Result	Stops	Qualifying Time	Grid
1	**Lewis Hamilton**	McLaren	1h39m09.440s	2	1m21.835s	4
2	**Nick Heidfeld**	BMW Sauber	1h40m18.017s	2	1m21.873s	5
3	**Rubens Barrichello**	Honda	1h40m31.713s	3	1m21.512s	16
4	**Kimi Raikkonen**	Ferrari	59 laps	2	1m21.706s	3
5	**Heikki Kovalainen**	McLaren	59 laps	2	1m21.049s	1
6	**Fernando Alonso**	Renault	59 laps	2	1m22.029s	6
7	**Jarno Trulli**	Toyota	59 laps	2	1m20.601s	14
8	**Kazuki Nakajima**	Williams	59 laps	2	1m21.112s	15
9	**Nico Rosberg**	Williams	59 laps	3	1m21.668s	20*
10	**Mark Webber**	Red Bull	59 laps	2	1m21.554s	2
11	**Sebastien Bourdais**	Toro Rosso	59 laps	2	1m20.531s	13
12	**Timo Glock**	Toyota	59 laps	2	1m20.274s	12
13	**Felipe Massa**	Ferrari	58 laps	3	1m23.305s	9
R	**Robert Kubica**	BMW Sauber	39 laps/spun off	2	No time	10
R	**Jenson Button**	Honda	38 laps/spun off	2	1m21.631s	17
R	**Nelson Piquet Jr**	Renault	35 laps/spun off	1	1m22.491s	7
R	**Giancarlo Fisichella**	Force India	26 laps/spun off	0	1m21.885s	19
R	**Adrian Sutil**	Force India	10 laps/spun off	0	1m21.786s	18
R	**Sebastian Vettel**	Toro Rosso	0 laps/spun off	0	1m23.251s	8
R	**David Coulthard**	Red Bull	0 laps/spun off	0	1m20.174s	11

FASTEST LAP: RAIKKONEN, 1M32.150S, 124.797MPH/200.842KPH ON LAP 18
RACE LEADERS: KOVALAINEN 1-4; HAMILTON 5-21, 23-60; HEIDFELD 22
* STARTED FROM THE PITLANE

TALKING POINT: BRITISH GP TO TURN ITS BACK ON SILVERSTONE

Bernie Ecclestone and Silverstone had long been at war, with the F1 boss's attacks on the circuit's owners, the British Racing Drivers' Club, part of the annual show. However, the bombshell he dropped on Silverstone as it celebrated the 60th anniversary of hosting the first British GP rocked it to the core. Negotiations had been ongoing, with the BRDC having got planning approval for the changes he'd been seeking. But then the news broke that, from 2010, Donington Park would host the race. Fans were relieved that Britain wouldn't lose its grand prix, but they were amazed, as Donington had much work to do to meet the standard required.

Conditions were foul, but the racing exciting in what might be Silverstone's penultimate grand prix.

GERMAN GP

Lewis Hamilton powered back into the lead of the title race in an event that should have been a walk in the park but turned into something considerably more difficult when McLaren appeared not to react to the arrival of the safety car.

Spot the similarity. In Canada, Lewis Hamilton started from pole position and led easily until the safety car was deployed. In Germany, Hamilton started from pole and led easily until the safety car was deployed.

Spot the difference. In Canada, Hamilton messed up in the pits, ending up with no points. In Germany, Hamilton was left with a mountain to climb after being instructed not to pit under the safety car, as a result having to open out a 23s advantage in eight laps over Felipe Massa before he pitted to be sure of emerging still in the lead. He didn't quite manage this, coming back out from his second pit stop in fifth position but he still went on to win. So, it was a case of zero in one, hero in the other.

The safety car came out because Timo Glock's Toyota broke away from him at the final corner, because the right rear tyre came off his car after the suspension collapsed, and slammed into the pit wall, scattering debris. He spent the night in hospital, but was back out testing four days later.

At the start of the race, Hamilton rocketed into the lead, with Massa delayed slightly as he fought off a challenge from Heikki Kovalainen. This is how they would run to the first round of pit stops, with Hamilton 11s clear when he came in on lap 18.

This was earlier than his rivals, and he was joined in the pits by Robert Kubica who had leapt from seventh to fourth on lap 1.

After Hamilton and, two laps later, Massa had resumed in first and second places, third position was being held down by Glock, who had yet to make his pit stop.

The German's spell in this lofty position may have pleased the home crowd who were hoping that one of their five nationals would deliver, but it quickly came to nothing when he pitted at mid-distance and dropped back behind Kovalainen, Kubica, Kimi Raikkonen, Jarno Trulli and Sebastian Vettel.

When Glock triggered the safety car's deployment, Hamilton had opened his lead back out to 12s. Kovalainen was running third, 6s further back. At this point, Nick Heidfeld, who had started 12th, had not long pitted and was fuelled for a long second stint. This was to prove a masterstroke as he was elevated from 10th to second when everyone bar Hamilton pitted after the pit lane opened during the safety car period.

Lewis Hamilton drives his McLaren inside Nelson Piquet Jr's Renault to score a brilliant fighgtback victory to open out his championship points lead.

This was absolutely nothing next to the transformation that befell Nelson Piquet Jr's race. It all appeared to have got away from him when he was able to qualify only 17th, but it all came back when his race was transformed by making his only planned stop just as the safety car was summoned. Amazingly, Piquet Jr ended up second, having overtaken just one driver, Kazuki Nakajima. And that was when the Williams driver spun... Piquet Jr even led for six laps when Hamilton made his second pit stop. Never before had anyone benefitted from a safety car in such spectacular fashion.

Hamilton had had to have the hammer down before his second stop and had made up 16 of the 23s required. After his stop, he kept on driving right on the edge, as he chased and then was let past by team-mate Kovalainen. Two laps later, Heidfeld made his second stop and ceded the lead to Piquet.

Hamilton then hunted down Massa and scythed by the Ferrari at the hairpin with nonchalant ease as the Brazilian struggled with his braking. Three laps later, Hamilton's work was done as he forced Piquet Jr to accept the inevitable and took the lead, again making his move into the hairpin.

The Renault driver kept calm and landed that career best second place, with Massa a very dispirited third, just resisting Heidfeld.

HOCKENHEIM ROUND 10
Date: **20 July 2008** Laps: **67** Distance: **190.433 miles/306.458km**
Weather: **Cloudy and warm**

RACE RESULT

Position	Driver	Team	Result	Stops	Qualifying Time	Grid
1	**Lewis Hamilton**	McLaren	1h31m20.874s	2	1m15.666s	1
2	**Nelson Piquet Jr**	Renault	1h31m26.460s	1	1m16.189s	17
3	**Felipe Massa**	Ferrari	1h31m30.213s	2	1m15.859s	2
4	**Nick Heidfeld**	BMW Sauber	1h31m30.699s	2	1m15.581s	12
5	**Heikki Kovalainen**	McLaren	1h31m33.285s	2	1m16.143s	3
6	**Kimi Raikkonen**	Ferrari	1h31m35.357s	2	1m16.389s	6
7	**Robert Kubica**	BMW Sauber	1h31m43.477s	2	1m16.521s	7
8	**Sebastian Vettel**	Toro Rosso	1h31m54.156s	2	1m17.244s	9
9	**Jarno Trulli**	Toyota	1h31m58.073s	2	1m16.191s	4
10	**Niko Rosberg**	Williams	1h31m58.532s	2	1m15.633s	13
11	**Fernando Alonso**	Renault	1h31m59.499s	2	1m16.385s	5
12	**Sebastien Bourdais**	Toro Rosso	1h31m59.985s	2	1m15.858s	15
13	**David Coulthard**	Red Bull	1h32m15.845s	2	1m17.503s	10
14	**Kazuki Nakajima**	Williams	1h32m20.877s	2	1m16.083s	16
15	**Adrian Sutil**	Force India	1h32m30.362s	2	1m16.657s	19
16	**Giancarlo Fisichella**	Force India	1h32m44.967s*	2	1m16.963s	20
17	**Jenson Button**	Honda	66 laps	3	1m15.701s	14
R	**Rubens Barrichello**	Honda	50 laps/accident damage	2	1m16.246s	18
R	**Mark Webber**	Red Bull	40 laps/oil cooler	2	1m17.014s	8
R	**Timo Glock**	Toyota	35 laps/accident	1	1m15.508s	11

FASTEST LAP: HEIDFELD, 1M15.987S, 134.651MPH/216.700KPH ON LAP 52
RACE LEADERS: HAMILTON 1-18,22-37, 39-50, 60-67; MASSA 19-20, 38; KOVALAINEN 21; HEIDFELD 51-53; PIQUET JR 54-59
* INCLUDES A 25S PENALTY FOR UNLAPPING HIMSELF BEHIND THE SAFETY CAR BEFORE BEING SIGNALLED TO DO SO

TALKING POINT: SEBASTIAN VETTEL HAILED AS GERMANY'S HERO

When David Coulthard announced that his time in F1 would stop at the end of 2008, everyone reckoned that Sebastian Vettel would be promoted from the Scuderia Toro Rosso sister team to Red Bull Racing. They were right, with the just-turned-21-year-old being given the nod before his home race. Some hailed him as the "next Schumacher", something that wouldn't be far-fetched in terms of talent, as shown by his rise through the junior formulae, but not everyone was at this point picking him out as a future champion. For now, though, the German crowds love him, anxious that at least one of their five F1 drivers in 2008 will make it to the top.

Sebastian Vettel was seen as promising, a great hope, but his first win in Monza would change that.

HUNGARIAN GP

Everyone predicted that Lewis Hamilton would walk this race, but Felipe Massa blasted past the pole-sitter into Turn 1 and went on to control proceedings, only to have his engine fail, giving the glory to first-time winner Heikki Kovalainen.

Felipe Massa pulls off the move of the race to take the lead from Lewis Hamilton around the outside of the first turn. But it wasn't to be his day.

This was a strange one, a race that upset the form book, was peppered with incidents and then produced a new winner with a major shock just three laps from the finish.

Everything had been pointing to glory for Hamilton, the McLaren driver arriving on a roll after his wins at Silverstone and Hockenheim. Fastest in the second and third practice sessions, then appreciably better than his rivals in qualifying. Add to this the fact that the Hungaroring offers such a paucity of places to overtake, and it looked as though 10 points would be coming his way. Especially so, as his McLaren team-mate Heikki Kovalainen was next fastest in qualifying, with Felipe Massa the best of the rest for Ferrari in third, while Robert Kubica, the fast-improving Timo Glock for the ever-

improving Toyota team and Kimi Raikkonen completed the top-six.

Few thought that Massa would be able to offer much of a challenge, especially after his less than impressive or aggressive runs in the previous two grands prix. But then, as he had done before at the start of the 2006 and 2007 seasons, he followed two poor performances with a beauty, raising the question as to whether he needs to get angry to realise his potential.

Starting on the clean side of the circuit, Massa made a brilliant getaway from third, popping out of Hamilton's slipstream to the outside going into Turn 1, locking up and still managing to go around the outside, showing the sort of aggression that you'd expect to see from Hamilton, not him. Then,

again confounding predictions, he was able to pull away, with Glock getting immediately into fourth position behind Kovalainen and easily holding off Raikkonen.

The big question was what fuel load they were carrying, and Massa was duly the first of the frontrunners to pit, albeit only a lap before Hamilton, with Kovalainen coming in a further two laps later. Their order was re-established and again Hamilton didn't have an answer to Massa's pace.

Then Hamilton ran wide at Turn 1 on lap 41, his front left tyre having punctured. He had been 5s behind, losing out slightly to Massa, suffering with his tyres and now he had to limp all the way back to the pits, emerging in 10th place on a new set of tyres and now fuelled to the end, knowing that he would have to fly to salvage any points.

Massa made his final pit stop three laps later, fully four laps before Kovalainen, and was comfortably in the lead afterwards. But then his engine blew as he started the 68th of the 70 laps...Perhaps Massa's finest drive of the year was to go unrewarded and Kovalainen was duly a delighted recipient of victory, which was his first and made him the 100th driver to win a grand prix.

Glock's performance was inspired, coming a fortnight after his big crash in Germany, and he resisted a late-race charge from Raikkonen to claim second. That Raikkonen was challenging him troubled Renault, as he had been behind Alonso before the second round of pit stops, made a mistake on his in-lap, yet still emerged ahead.

Alonso went on to finish 5s adrift in fourth, one place ahead of Hamilton.

Piquet Jr was in the points for a third race in a row, proving his discovery of form wasn't temporary, while Jarno Trulli made it a doubly good day for Toyota.

The final point went to Kubica, who lost four places at his first pit stop and was less than impressed by BMW Sauber's slide away from the pace. Team-mate Nick Heidfeld failed to move on from first qualifying and his attempted one-stop race strategy enabled him to climb only as high as 10th.

HUNGARORING ROUND 11

Date: **3 August 2008** Laps: **70** Distance: **190.540 miles/306.645km**
Weather: **Hot & dry**

RACE RESULT

Position	Driver	Team	Result	Stops	Qualifying Time	Grid
1	Heikki Kovalainen	McLaren	1h37m27.067s	2	1m21.140s	2
2	Timo Glock	Toyota	1h37m38.128s	2	1m21.326s	5
3	Kimi Raikkonen	Ferrari	1h37m43.923s	2	1m21.516s	6
4	Fernando Alonso	Renault	1h37m48.681s	2	1m21.698s	7
5	Lewis Hamilton	McLaren	1h37m50.115s	2	1m20.899s	1
6	Nelson Piquet Jr	Renault	1h37m59.365s	2	1m22.371s	10
7	Jarno Trulli	Toyota	1h38m03.516s	2	1m21.767s	9
8	Robert Kubica	BMW Sauber	1h38m15.388s	2	1m21.281s	4
9	Mark Webber	Red Bull	1h38m25.901s	2	1m21.732s	8
10	Nick Heidfeld	BMW Sauber	1h38m34.776s	1	1m21.045s	15
11	David Coulthard	Red Bull	1h38m37.474s	2	1m20.502s	13
12	Jenson Button	Honda	69 laps	2	1m20.332s	12
13	Kazuki Nakajima	Williams	69 laps	1	1m21.085s	16
14	Nico Rosberg	Williams	69 laps	2	No time	14
15	Giancarlo Fisichella	Force India	69 laps	2	1m21.670s	18
16	Rubens Barrichello	Honda	68 laps	2	1m21.332s	17
17	Felipe Massa	Ferrari	67 laps/engine	2	1m21.191s	3
18	Sebastien Bourdais	Toro Rosso	67 laps	3	1m20.963s	19
R	Adrian Sutil	Force India	62 laps/brakes	3	1m22.113s	20
R	Sebastian Vettel	Toro Rosso	22 laps/engine	1	1m20.144s	11

FASTEST LAP: RAIKKONEN, 1M21.195S, 120.697MPH/194.243KPH ON LAP 61
RACE LEADERS: MASSA 1- 18, 22-44, 49-67; HAMILTON 19; KOVALAINEN 20-21, 45-48, 68-70
* 5-PLACE GRID PENALTY FOR IMPEDING HEIDFELD

TALKING POINT: GETTING HOT UNDER THE COLLAR IN THE PITS

One refuelling fire a year is above average, so the teams were perplexed that three cars caught fire in Hungary. Sebastien Bourdais was the first to be afflicted, at the first of his two stops, though he was soon sent back into the race. Rubens Barrichello was next to have fuel catch light around his car, this after a problem with Honda's refuelling rig. Then Kazuki Nakajima's Williams caught light when he left his second stop. Teams suggested the fires might have happened because of high ambient temperatures leading to fuel expanding in the hose and coming out with a greater pressure than normal. Post-race investigation came up with no answers.

Bourdais, Barrichello and Nakajima all escaped without injury after brief fires during refuelling.

EUROPEAN GP

Small moments can turn an entire year and Felipe Massa had one of those on Formula One's first visit to Valencia when his Ferrari was waved away from a pit stop into the path of another car in the pits and got away without a time penalty.

Felipe Massa leads into the first corner and it was very much his show from then on, with only a scare in the pit lane to worry him.

This incident in the pit lane came when the Ferrari driver had the race under control, leading with ease from Lewis Hamilton. It was Massa's second pit stop, on lap 37 out of 57, and the rush was unnecessary bearing in mind his lead was more than 10 seconds, but he was released from his stop to run alongside Adrian Sutil's Force India for much of the remainder of the pit lane before backing off as it narrowed. There was concern that Ferrari might have earned him a drive-through penalty and so gifted the race to Hamilton. Yet, after a wait while the stewards deliberated, Massa escaped censure and Ferrari was hit instead with a Euro 10,000 fine.

To get to this stage, Massa found fine form on Formula One's first visit to this new Spanish circuit that snaked around Valencia's docks. He took pole by 0.21 seconds from Hamilton and used all of the Ferrari's impressive speed down the straights to break clear.

Hamilton had had to have pain-killing injections to calm a neck spasm and so was relieved to keep Robert Kubica back in third as they dived into the first tight corner. The BMW Sauber then had no answer to his pace and so at least Hamilton was able thereafter to concentrate on his own race.

The fact that it was Kubica in third rather than Kimi Raikkonen for Ferrari or Heikki Kovalainen for McLaren speaks volumes for the Pole, but the relative lack of developmental progress made by BMW Sauber was clear for all to see and his somewhat fortuitous Hamilton-assisted victory in Canada seemed a long time ago. By race's end, he was still third, but 37 seconds down on Massa. Team-mate Nick Heidfeld could only hang his head in embarrassment as his continued difficulty in qualifying well led to him starting eighth and finishing out of the points in ninth.

Kovalainen started with a heavy fuel load and made his most important move at the start when he got ahead of Raikkonen, but there was nothing he could do about Kubica. Raikkonen was out of sorts all meeting and was nowhere near team-mate Massa's pace when running fifth before having an engine failure similar to Massa's in the Hungarian GP. He also knocked over one of his pit crew.

This promoted Jarno Trulli to fifth and Timo Glock showed Toyota's continued progress by claiming seventh.

Between them, Sebastian Vettel bagged sixth, matching his grid position and emphasizing how much progress Scuderia Toro Rosso had made. The fact that it was way ahead of its parent team, Red Bull Racing, was thought to be largely down to its Ferrari engines in its chassis being superior to the Renault V8s in the RB4s. Speed trap figures showed that the Toro Rossos were ahead of all but the Ferraris, but the advancement was clear to the naked eye. Indeed, Vettel had been fastest of all in the first practice session and Sebastien Bourdais fourth. Bourdais didn't end up with points, but his run to 10th was more competitive even than when he collected two points in the Australian GP, a race of considerable attrition.

The final point went to Nico Rosberg and it was his first since the Turkish GP as Williams struggled to find form. Team-mate Kazuki Nakajima made himself the most unpopular driver with the crowds, as he failed to brake in time as Heidfeld rejoined the track after an incident at the start with Bourdais and slammed into the back of none other than Fernando Alonso, ripping off the Renault's rear wing.

VALENCIA ROUND 12

Date: **24 August 2008** Laps: **57** Distance: **191.919 miles/308.864km**
Weather: **Sunny and warm**

RACE RESULT

Position	Driver	Team	Result	Stops	Qualifying Time	Grid
1	Felipe Massa	Ferrari	1h35m32.339s	2	1m38.989s	1
2	Lewis Hamilton	McLaren	1h35m37.950s	2	1m39.199s	2
3	Robert Kubica	BMW Sauber	1h36m09.692s	2	1m39.392s	3
4	Heikki Kovalainen	McLaren	1h36m12.042s	2	1m39.937s	5
5	Jarno Trulli	Toyota	1h36m23.023s	2	1m40.309s	7
6	Sebastian Vettel	Toro Rosso	1h36m24.964s	2	1m40.142s	6
7	Timo Glock	Toyota	1h36m40.329s	1	1m38.499s	13
8	Nico Rosberg	Williams	1h36m43.796s	2	1m40.721s	9
9	Nick Heidfeld	BMW Sauber	1h36m54.516s	2	1m40.631s	8
10	Sebastien Bourdais	Toro Rosso	1h37m02.133s	2	1m40.750s	10
11	Nelson Piquet Jr	Renault	1h37m05.056s	1	1m38.744s	15
12	Mark Webber	Red Bull	56 laps	1	1m38.515s	14
13	Jenson Button	Honda	56 laps	1	1m38.880s	16
14	Giancarlo Fisichella	Force India	56 laps	1	1m39.268s	18
15	Kazuki Nakajima	Williams	56 laps	2	1m38.428s	11
16	Rubens Barrichello	Honda	56 laps	1	1m39.811s	19*
17	David Coulthard	Red Bull	56 laps	2	1m39.235s	17
R	Kimi Raikkonen	Ferrari	45 laps/engine	2	1m39.488s	4
R	Adrian Sutil	Force India	41 laps/spun off	2	1m39.943s	20*
R	Fernando Alonso	Renault	0 laps/collision	0	1m38.435s	12

FASTEST LAP: MASSA, 1M38.708S, 124.039MPH/199.621KPH ON LAP 36
RACE LEADERS: MASSA 1-14, 20-36, 39-57; HAMILTON 15-16, 37-38; KUBICA 17; KOVALAINEN 18-19
* STARTED FROM THE PIT LANE

TALKING POINT: WAS THE NEW VALENCIA CIRCUIT A HIT?

Going racing at a new venue is always fun and there was much anticipation for what Hermann Tilke had produced around Valencia's docks. The area had been boosted by hosting the America's Cup yachting event, but was still some way short of the glamour of Monaco. Indeed, Ron Dennis suggested that more yachts in the harbour would help. The drivers liked the flow, finding it a challenge. But, as ever, it took an Australian to cut to the chase, with Mark Webber saying "it was quite good to drive, but it was sh*t for racing". The fans would concur and a redesign with a longer straight was suggested by some, while others wanted more low-speed corners.

The outline of the new circuit can be seen from this high shot over Valencia's harbour district.

BELGIAN GP

Every so often, usually when rain strikes, a grand prix can be transformed and the final laps in Belgium produced spell-binding action as drivers teetered on the brink. Through it all came Lewis Hamilton to win. But then he was given a time penalty...

Lewis Hamilton hassles Kimi Raikkonen into Les Combes after chucking away at La Source at the start of lap 2. They would battle all race.

Grabbing pole position at Spa-Francorchamps is a feather in any driver's hat, but it was more than that for Lewis Hamilton. The English driver had been confident going to Belgium, and this was the proof.

Hamilton led away, with Kimi Raikkonen going from fourth to third as Heikki Kovalainen clashed with Nick Heidfeld at the hairpin. He then got a better exit from Eau Rouge than team-mate Felipe Massa and relieved him of second place at Les Combes. Less than a lap later, Hamilton spun at La Source. Fortunately for the McLaren driver, he hooked a gear and accelerated down the hill still in front, but Raikkonen had greater momentum and used it to take the lead at Les Combes.

This is how they stayed through the first and second rounds of pit stops, with Massa a distant third. But then, oh yes, Spa-Francorchamps received a little of its holy water. Yup, rain fell with three laps to go. And now we had a race on our hands, as Raikkonen's Ferrari looked decidedly short on grip. Hamilton had been closing in, more in hope than expectation, and now he was gaining hand over fist.

The moment that was to decide the outcome of the race came at the Bus Stop chicane. Having been faster up the climb from Blanchimont, Hamilton had the momentum. Combine this with the fact that Raikkonen was being cautious, unsure of how much wetter the track would be, and Hamilton seized his moment. On the outside line, he got half a

car's length ahead. But Raikkonen refused to back off and drove a wide exit out of the right-hand part of the sequence, giving Hamilton the slim option of backing off or running over the kerbs. He took the latter and rejoined in front. Knowing that he had to cede the position, he let Raikkonen retake the lead as they crossed the start/finish line, tucked in behind and then dived up the inside into La Source.

If this was excitement enough for most, there was more to follow as Raikkonen fought back. Powering into Pouhon, now more slippery than before, both ran wide at the double left-hander. Raikkonen stayed on the run-off all the way to its end and was faster into Fagnes, where Hamilton was confronted by Nico Rosberg's Williams as it returned to the track.

He darted left in avoidance and Raikkonen grabbed the moment to dive between the two and regain the lead. Moments later, Raikkonen spun back to second. This was fabulous.

Raikkonen then made an error at Blanchimont and went off to the right, then spun across the track and hit the wall.

Onto the final lap, Massa wasn't gaining, so Hamilton ought to have been safe, but it was now a deluge. His final lap was almost a minute slower than his best, but it was enough. And victory was his, for a while...

Massa trailed him home, 14s in arrears, but Heidfeld showed what could be done by those who pitted for rain tyres, climbing from ninth to third in just two laps. Fernando Alonso was next home, cursing himself for not pitting until the end of lap 43, aware that had he pitted on lap 42, he might even have passed Massa.

Sebastian Vettel and Robert Kubica – who wasn't able to pit on lap 42 as he'd been behind Heidfeld on the track and didn't want to queue up behind his team-mate in the pits – passed Sebastien Bourdais on the final lap for fifth and sixth places.

Long after the podium celebrations, Hamilton was adjudged to have gained an advantage by cutting the chicane and given a 25s penalty, dropping him to third and reducing his points advantage to just two over surprised winner Massa.

SPA-FRANCORCHAMPS ROUND 13

Date: **7 September 2008** Laps: **44** Distance: **191.491 miles/308.175km**
Weather: **Warm and damp**

Position	Driver	Team	Result	Stops	Qualifying Time	Grid
1	**Felipe Massa**	Ferrari	1h22m59.394s	2	1m47.678s	2
2	**Nick Heidfeld**	BMW Sauber	1h2m08.777s	3	1m48.315s	5
3	**Lewis Hamilton**	McLaren	1h23m09.933s*	2	1m47.338s	1
4	**Fernando Alonso**	Renault	1h23m13.872s	3	1m48.504s	6
5	**Sebastian Vettel**	Toro Rosso	1h23m13.970s	2	1m50.319s	10
6	**Robert Kubica**	BMW Sauber	1h23m14.431s	2	1m48.763s	8
7	**Sebastien Bourdais**	Toro Rosso	1h23m16.129s	2	1m48.951s	9
8	**Mark Webber**	Red Bull	1h23m42.170s	2	1m48.736s	7
9	**Timo Glock**	Toyota	1h24m06.439s*	2	1m46.995s	13
10	**Heikki Kovalainen**	McLaren	43 laps	3	1m47.815s	3
11	**David Coulthard**	Red Bull	43 laps	2	1m47.018s	14
12	**Nico Rosberg**	Williams	43 laps	2	1m47.429s	15
13	**Adrian Sutil**	Force India	43 laps	2	1m48.226s	18
14	**Kazuki Nakajima**	Williams	43 laps	2	1m48.268s	19
15	**Jenson Button**	Honda	43 laps	2	1m48.211s	17
16	**Jarno Trulli**	Toyota	43 laps	2	1m46.949s	11
17	**Giancarlo Fisichella**	Force India	43 laps	3	1m48.447s	20
18	**Kimi Raikkonen**	Ferrari	42 laps/spun off	2	1m47.992s	4
R	**Rubens Barrichello**	Honda	19 laps/gearbox	1	1m48.153s	16
R	**Nelson Piquet Jr**	Renault	13 laps/spun off	0	1m46.965s	12

FASTEST LAP: RAIKKONEN, 1M47.930S, 145.163MPH/233.618KPH ON LAP 24
RACE LEADERS: HAMILTON 1, 43-44; RAIKKONEN, 2-12, 14-25, 29-42; MASSA 13, 26-28
* INCLUDES 25S TIME PENALTY ADDED

TALKING POINT: JUST WHO ARE THE STEWARDS?

Feathers were ruffled by the stewards' decision to give Lewis Hamilton a 25s penalty. Whether the trio of stewards were right or wrong, the matter that was most widely debated was whether the stewards were qualified for the job rather than whether, as most drivers reckoned, that Lewis had gained a slight advantage through his actions. The panel for the Belgian GP were Yves Bacquelaine (Belgium), Nicholas Deschaux (France) and Surinder Thatthi (Kenya), with a completely different panel for each of the year's grands prix. The swell of opinion was that permanent stewards should be appointed to apply the sport's laws with consistency.

McLaren made a trip to an FIA hearing in Paris, only to hear that its appeal was inadmissible.

ITALIAN GP

Think about this. Sebastian Vettel became the youngest ever grand prix winner, at the age of just 21. He did so in streaming wet conditions, never putting a foot wrong. And he did it in a car run by a team that just a few years before was regular tail-ender, Minardi.

Sebastian Vettel kicks up the spray as he races to both his and Toro Rosso's first win.

chassis. Yet, thanks to Vettel's genial nature and his obvious enthusiasm, everyone was happy to celebrate the moment and welcome another potential World Champion to the top step of the podium.

For Monza, read monsoon. Rain had been forecast, but few had predicted that it would last for three days. Vettel didn't appear to care, though, and really delivered in qualifying. The Toro Rosso STR03 was clearly right on it, as Bourdais ended up fourth fastest, sandwiching McLaren's Heikki Kovalainen and Red Bull's Mark Webber.

By contrast, championship contenders Felipe Massa and Lewis Hamilton qualified sixth and 15th. Hamilton and McLaren had made too bold a bid in the second qualifying session, fitting intermediates, only for it to rain harder. He was sunk. Kimi Raikkonen also fumbled and would start 14th.

Race officials decided that it was too wet for a normal start, so sent the field off behind the safety car. This pulled off after two laps, having made Vettel's day easier, as he was thus protected from attack on the run to the first chicane, with Kovalainen and the rest of the field blinded by his spray. Vettel didn't put a foot wrong.

Certainly, he had qualified light and made his first pit stop four laps before the next three drivers behind him did. They were Kovalainen, Webber and Massa. Yet, when they rejoined, Vettel was back in front and his main concern turned to those who were running a one-stop strategy. Of these, Nico Rosberg was best placed, but Hamilton was closing in fast and was soon past the Williams driver to run second, closing to within 1.1s of Vettel on lap 26. Amazingly,

Twenty-one years and 73 days old, and with a smile a mile wide. That was Sebastian Vettel after the race at Monza. That was the man/boy who clambered from his Toro Rosso and punched the air with delight. That was the driver who was cheered to the rafters by a team made up of engineers and mechanics who had spent decades treating the occasional point as a miracle when the

team raced as Minardi. And, whisper it, that was the driver who had taken victory with a Ferrari engine, in Italy, with the two Ferrari drivers far behind in his wake.

Certainly, there was talk that Vettel and his team-mate Sebastien Bourdais had been powered by Ferrari engines sporting development parts and so ought to be fast, especially in their Adrian Newey-designed from 15th on the grid, the race could be his.

McLaren elected not to gamble when he came in for his one planned stop on lap 27 and sent Hamilton back out on extreme wets. You could forgive them, as their gamble in qualifying had backfired.

Fortune wasn't with Hamilton or Rosberg as it was only a lap or so after they pitted that it became clear that intermediate tyres would be the ones to have and that they would have to pit again.

This dropped Hamilton to seventh place when he pitted on lap 36, but he instantly picked off Mark Webber. Rosberg didn't even wait that long to pit, but he dropped right down the order.

With clear evidence that intermediate tyres were much faster in the conditions, Vettel had them fitted when he pitted for the second time on lap 36, and the race was his, beating Kovalainen by 12.5s.

Any concern that Hamilton would mount a further charge was extinguished when he rooted his tyres by pushing too hard and he was to rise no higher than seventh. Luckily for him, that was only one place behind Massa, so his points advantage was trimmed to just one point.

The day, though, belonged to Vettel and everyone at Scuderia Toro Rosso who had fought so long and hard for so little.

MONZA ROUND 14

Date: **14 September 2008** Laps: **53** Distance: **190.779 miles/307.029km** Weather: **Wet then overcast**

Position	Driver	Team	Result	Stops	Qualifying Time	Grid
1	Sebastian Vettel	Toro Rosso	1h26m47.494s	2	1m37.555s	1
2	Heikki Kovalainen	McLaren	1h27m00.006s	2	1m37.631s	2
3	Robert Kubica	BMW Sauber	1h27m07.965s	1	1m36.697s	11
4	Fernando Alonso	Renault	1h27m11.397s	1	1m39.751s	8
5	Nick Heidfeld	BMW Sauber	1h27m15.242s	1	1m39.906s	10
6	Felipe Massa	Ferrari	1h27m16.310s	2	1m38.894s	6
7	Lewis Hamilton	McLaren	1h27m17.406s	2	1m39.625s	15
8	Mark Webber	Red Bull	1h27m19.542s	2	1m38.117s	3
9	Kimi Raikkonen	Ferrari	1h27m26.962s	2	1m37.522s	14
10	Nelson Piquet Jr	Renault	1h27m41.939s	1	1m36.630s	17
11	Timo Glock	Toyota	1h27m46.382s	2	1m39.787s	9
12	Kazuki Nakajima	Williams	1h27m49.509s	1	1m36.653s	18*
13	Jarno Trulli	Toyota	1h27m53.448s	2	1m39.152s	7
14	Nico Rosberg	Williams	1h27m56.129s	2	1m38.767s	5
15	Jenson Button	Honda	1h28m00.864s	2	1m37.006s	19*
16	David Coulthard	Red Bull	52 laps	2	1m37.284s	13
17	Rubens Barrichello	Honda	52 laps	2	1m36.510s	16
18	Sebastien Bourdais	Toro Rosso	52 laps	2	1m38.445s	4
19	Adrian Sutil	Force India	51 laps	3	1m37.417s	20
R	Giancarlo Fisichella	Force India	11 laps/accident	0	1m36.698s	12

FASTEST LAP: RAIKKONEN, 1M28.047S, 147.194MPH/236.886KPH ON LAP 53
RACE LEADERS: VETTEL 1-18, 23-53; KOVALAINEN 19-22

TALKING POINT: VETTEL IS THE YOUNGEST AT EVERYTHING

Sebastian Vettel left almost no age records standing after his blitz at Monza. He had already become the youngest driver to drive in a grand prix when he made his debut as BMW Sauber's third driver in 2006. He went on to become the youngest driver to make his grand prix racing debut, at 19 years and 348 days, also becoming the youngest points scorer on that debut. Taking pole at Monza broke another record – Alonso's – by almost a year and his win took a similar amount off the mark for youngest winner set by Alonso in 2003. His next target is Hamilton's record as youngest World Champion.

Old enough to be a grand prix winner, but young enough to be thrown around by his team...

SINGAPORE GP

In life, you take what comes your way and Fernando Alonso did just that, with a strategy forced on him by mechanical failure that left him 15th and by his car's appetite for brakes. All it needed was for Piquet to bring out the safety car...

Formula One night racing is go, as Lewis Hamilton's McLaren leads the chase after Ferrari pole-sitter Felipe Massa who is already out of shot.

Formula One's first night race was a revelation. However, the main thing for which it will be remembered is how a driver who started 15th won, thanks to a twist of fate.

This was Fernando Alonso and the arrival of the safety car put him into an all but untouchable position in a race that ought to have gone to Ferrari's Felipe Massa or McLaren's Lewis Hamilton. Without the safety car's deployment, Renault's Spanish ace would have been hard pushed even to reach a point-scoring position.

The irony of this upturn in form is that Alonso's R28 was fastest in the second and third practice sessions. Then all dreams of pole position were scuppered when a fuel hose came adrift before he could set a time in second qualifying, leaving him 15th.

This was when the team decided that the R28 was eating the super-soft tyres and so Alonso would run a short first stint on them before changing to the regular soft rubber. This, though, is not the accepted way to make up ground as most would go for a one-stop strategy and run for as long as possible before coming in so that they could get past slower cars that had started ahead.

Massa led from pole, keeping Hamilton in his wake and Kimi Raikkonen third ahead of Robert Kubica, with Heikki Kovalainen's challenge at Turn 3 leading to him losing places to Sebastian Vettel and Timo Glock.

Alonso reached 12th on lap 1 by passing Mark Webber, Jenson Button and David Coulthard. He then passed Jarno Trulli after being delayed by his Toyota for seven laps.

On lap 12, he pitted and fell to the tail.

The race turned on its head just as Raikkonen started catching Hamilton by Nelson Piquet Jr crashing and bringing out the safety car. Keke Rosberg and Kubica had their races ruined as they were both so low on fuel that they had to pit when the pitlane was closed, thus being hit with drivethrough penalties. When the pits opened on lap 17, in came the rest bar the one-stopping Trulli and Force India's Giancarlo Fisichella.

Alonso, having gained his pitstop for nothing due to the bunching of the field, was fifth by the time the safety car withdrew.

Raikkonen lost time queuing behind Massa, with this being made far worse when Massa was signalled via his steering wheel traffic lights to leave too soon and left with his fuel hose still attached, knocking down two of his crew. This left mechanics bruised, Raikkonen 17th and Massa 19th as he had to wait for his mechanics to sprint to the pit exit to recover the hose.

Rosberg found himself in the lead, but he knew that he'd have to bring his Williams in to serve his drivethrough penalty. When he did, Trulli took over before coming in for his only stop. This left Alonso in front, with one more stop to make like every other frontrunner. Without showing race-winning speed or incision, the race was his.

Rosberg emerged in second, so his penalty hadn't hampered him that much, with Coulthard rising to third ahead of Hamilton. Red Bull had already hit trouble with Mark Webber losing what could have been second when his gearbox failed and then Coulthard lost three places with a slow second pit stop.

Once released from behind Coulthard, Hamilton closed in on Raikkonen, who still had to pit, but Adrian Sutil crashed his Force India, and so Hamilton closed the gap to Rosberg as the safety car came out again. Hamilton suppressed thoughts of making a do-or-die move when it pulled off and elected to cruise and collect, knowing that Massa was out of the points. Ferrari's bad day was compounded when Raikkonen crashed with four laps to go when chasing Glock.

SINGAPORE ROUND 15

Date: **28 September 2008** Laps: **61** Distance: **191.972 miles/ 308.950km** Weather: **Hot and dark**

Position	Driver	Team	Result	Stops	Qualifying Time	Grid
1	**Fernando Alonso**	Renault	1h57m16.304s	2	no time	15
2	**Nico Rosberg**	Williams	1h57m19.261s	3	1m46.611s	8
3	**Lewis Hamilton**	McLaren	1h57m22.221s	2	1m45.463s	2
4	**Timo Glock**	Toyota	1h57m24.459s	2	1m46.328s	7
5	**Sebastian Vettel**	Toro Rosso	1h57m26.572s	2	1m46.244s	6
6	**Nick Heidfeld**	BMW Sauber	1h57m27.405s	2	1m45.964s	9*
7	**David Coulthard**	Red Bull	1h57m32.691s	2	1m45.928s	14
8	**Kazuki Nakajima**	Williams	1h57m34.793s	2	1m47.547s	10
9	**Jenson Button**	Honda	1h57m36.189s	2	1m45.133s	12
10	**Heikki Kovalainen**	McLaren	1h57m43.206s	2	1m45.873s	5
11	**Robert Kubica**	BMW Sauber	1h57m44.279s	3	1m45.779s	4
12	**Sebastien Bourdais**	Toro Rosso	1h57m45.736s	2	1m46.389s	17
13	**Felipe Massa**	Ferrari	1h57m51.474s	2	1m44.801s	1
14	**Giancarlo Fisichella**	Force India	1h57m59.875s	1	no time	20**
15	**Kimi Raikkonen**	Ferrari	57 laps/accident	2	1m45.617s	3
R	**Jarno Trulli**	Toyota	50 laps/hydraulics	1	1m45.038s	11
R	**Adrian Sutil**	Force India	49 laps/accident	2	1m47.940s	19
R	**Mark Webber**	Red Bull	29 laps/gearbox	1	1m45.212s	13
R	**Rubens Barrichello**	Honda	14 laps/electrical	1	1m46.583s	18
R	**Nelson Piquet Jr**	Renault	13 laps/accident	0	1m46.037s	16

FASTEST LAP: RAIKKONEN, 1M45.59S, 107.358MPH/172.776KPH ON LAP 14
RACE LEADERS: MASSA 1-17; ROSBERG 18-28; TRULLI 29-33; ALONSO 34-61
* THREE-PLACE GRID PENALTY FOR IMPEDING BARRICHELLO IN Q1. ** STARTED FROM PIT LANE

TALKING POINT: NIGHT RACING IS A CONSIDERABLE HIT

TV viewers were thrilled by the sight of racing after dark. Singapore had done a brilliant job in building a track along its waterfront, with high-mounted camera positions showing how well lit the circuit was. The shot that showed buses motoring across a flyover was the pick of the crop. Sure, the circuit would be improved if more spots for overtaking could be added, but the unique backdrop made up for that. Sir Frank Williams suggested that it might take over from Monaco as the jewel in Formula One's crown. Years ago, this might have seemed heretical, but his sentiment was no doubt coloured by awareness of Singapore's economic value.

Singapore city centre provided a wonderful backdrop to Formula One's first ever night race.

JAPANESE GP

Lewis Hamilton made a poor start, lost his cool and attacked Kimi Raikkonen for the lead. It failed. He was penalised, but only after being spun by Felipe Massa. He too was penalised and Fernando Alonso scored a second straight victory.

There was considerable talk from Lewis Hamilton and McLaren before they headed to Japan that they weren't going to make the mistakes that cost them the 2007 drivers' title. No, they were going to play it safe and nurse their points advantage. That was understandable, but a racer is a racer and Hamilton was left to rue his response to his tardy getaway from pole position.

That the McLaren driver was starting from pole was to his credit as he had to dig deep to outsprint the Ferraris, earning accolades from all quarters as he found three-quarters of a second. Until then, it had been looking like an all-Ferrari front row. In a flash, Hamilton's title rival Felipe Massa found himself not second on the grid, but fifth as Heikki Kovalainen and Fernando Alonso also edged past.

This ought to have played into Hamilton's hands, starting four places ahead of Massa, but he panicked as Raikkonen got past him on the blast to the tight first corner. Using the Ferrari's slipstream, Hamilton thought in terms only of the corner not the race or especially the championship. He dived to the inside, found his tyres colder than expected, like almost all of his rivals, and slid wide. This forced Raikkonen wide and let Robert Kubica, up from sixth, into the lead.

The moment would lead to a drivethrough penalty for Hamilton, which was considerably more damaging than simply having accepted second place into the turn, and even worse was to follow...

Indeed, as Alonso followed Kubica out of the corner, with Kovalainen third and Hamilton fourth, the English driver ran wide at Turn 2, perhaps due to dirty tyres from his excursion, and in an instant he was back in sixth place, demoted by Jarno Trulli and Massa. Yes, the very driver he had been hoping to keep behind him.

Going onto lap 2, Hamilton closed in on Massa and then went for a move at Turn 11, the middle part of the Dunlop Corner chicane, when Massa appeared to outbrake himself, then came back across at him, tipping him into a spin. With flat-spotted tyres, Hamilton pitted and rejoined 19th, with only Kazuki Nakajima behind him after the Williams driver had damaged his nose against David

Lewis Hamilton caused havoc at the first corner when he ran wide and pushed Kimi Raikkonen et al onto the run-off, allowing Robert Kubica by.

Coulthard's Red Bull at the first corner. The Scot didn't even get that far, his suspension collapsing at Turn 2.

If Hamilton's mood was bad, think how thunderous it must have been on lap 17 when he was told that he'd been hit with a drivethrough penalty.

He wasn't alone, though, as Massa was given one too, and would come in for his from sixth place two laps later.

Hampered by a damaged floor, Hamilton was unable to rise higher than 12th as Alonso reached the front by making his first pit stop later than Kubica. The Pole finished 5s down in second, with Raikkonen lacklustre again, but able to collect his first points in five races for third place. The place, or better, should have gone to Kovalainen, but his engine failed.

It's said that Elf had helped Renault to 10bhp more by supplying upgraded oil, but that still doesn't take away from Nelson Piquet Jr's drive to fourth, with Jarno Trulli fifth.

For once, Sebastien Bourdais got one over Toro Rosso team-mate Sebastian Vettel, but the FIA decided that when Massa hit him as he exited the pit lane into Turn 1, it was the Frenchman's fault and added 25s to his race time, dropping Bourdais to 10th and promoting Vettel to sixth, Massa to seventh and Mark Webber to eighth. And so Hamilton's advantage fell to five points.

FUJI SPEEDWAY ROUND 16

Date: **12 October 2008** Laps: **67** Distance: **189.776 miles/305.416km**
Weather: **Cool and overcast**

RACE RESULT

Position	Driver	Team	Result	Stops	Qualifying Time	Grid
1	**Fernando Alonso**	Renault	1h30m21.892s	2	1m18.852s	4
2	**Robert Kubica**	BMW Sauber	1h30m27.175s	2	1m18.979s	6
3	**Kimi Raikkonen**	Ferrari	1h30m28.292s	2	1m18.644s	2
4	**Nelson Piquet Jr**	Renault	1h30m42.462s	2	1m18.274s	12
5	**Jarno Trulli**	Toyota	1h30m45.659s	2	1m19.026s	7
6	**Sebastian Vettel**	Toro Rosso	1h31m01.099s	2	1m19.638s	9
7	**Felipe Massa**	Ferrari	1h31m08.050s	3	1m18.874s	5
8	**Mark Webber**	Red Bull	1h31m12.703s	1	1m18.354s	13
9	**Nick Heidfeld**	BMW Sauber	1h31m16.012s	1	1m18.835s	16
10	**Sebastien Bourdais**	Toro Rosso	1h30m55.977s*	2	1m20.167s	10
11	**Nico Rosberg**	Williams	1h31m23.988s	1	1m18.672s	15
12	**Lewis Hamilton**	McLaren	1h31m40.792s	3	1m18.404s	1
13	**Rubens Barrichello**	Honda	66 laps	1	1m18.882s	17
14	**Jenson Button**	Honda	66 laps	1	1m19.100s	18
15	**Kazuki Nakajima**	Williams	66 laps	2	1m18.594s	14
R	**Giancarlo Fisichella**	Force India	21 laps/gearbox	0	1m19.910s	20
R	**Heikki Kovalainen**	McLaren	16 laps/engine	0	1m18.821s	3
R	**Adrian Sutil**	Force India	8 laps/tyre	0	1m19.163s	19
R	**Timo Glock**	Toyota	6 laps/crash damage	1	1m19.118s	8
R	**David Coulthard**	Red Bull	0 laps/accident	0	1m18.187s	11

FASTEST LAP: MASSA, 1M18.426S, 130.150MPH/209.456KPH ON LAP 55
RACE LEADERS: KUBICA 1-16, 44-45; ALONSO 17-18, 29-43, 53-67; TRULLI 19-21, 49; BOURDAIS 22-24; PIQUET 25-28, 50-52; RAIKKONEN 46-48
* 25S TIME PENALTY ADDED FOR COLLIDING WITH MASSA WHEN LEAVING PITS

TALKING POINT: CRASH PUTS CUSTOMER CARS BACK INTO FOCUS

If you thought talk of customer cars had been dispensed with, you are wrong as the economic crash brought focus onto the fact that a few teams might be on the verge of folding. With this in mind, as all taking part in Formula One know that the grid must be full or the wrong image will be sent out, discussions about customer cars reared their head, with Force India in conversation with McLaren. Ostensibly, this was about an engine supply deal, replacing its Ferrari V8s with Mercedes ones, but with customer chassis from the Woking team also being discussed. Part of the deal for Mercedes engines was thought to be a race seat for its protégé Paul di Resta.

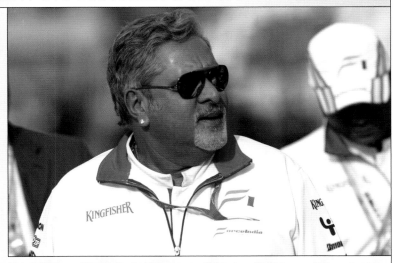

Force India owner Vijay Mallya had been in open discussion with McLaren and Mercedes.

CHINESE GP

Discipline was the key for Lewis Hamilton at Shanghai, scene of his denouement a year earlier. This he managed to display, along with great speed, to leave rival Felipe Massa a despondent second after being let through by his team-mate.

What's the best way to deflect criticism? To ram it back down your critics' throats, and this is what Lewis Hamilton did in China. Big time! The world and his dog, it seemed, was having a pop at him, calling him big-headed and overly aggressive out on the track. He couldn't take the pressure either, they said. Looking at his first corner antics in Japan, they might have had a point, but Hamilton's driving did the talking in Shanghai, silencing critics Fernando Alonso, Robert Kubica and even Flavio Briatore.

Fastest in both practice sessions on the Friday, he ended up second behind Nick Heidfeld on the Saturday then bounced back with an improved final run in the third qualifying session to take his seventh pole of the season. Now all he had to do to increase Ferrari's pain was to get down to the first corner in the lead and take it from there.

And this is what Hamilton did after making what he described as one of the best starts of his career. Title rival Felipe Massa was third on the grid and third into the first corner behind team-mate Kimi Raikkonen. Fleetingly, though, it looked as though Heikki Kovalainen might demote him, but the second McLaren driver had to back off and complete his demotion of Alonso for fourth. Alonso didn't like this one little bit and made a better exit from Turn 13 to pull alongside as they came onto the back straight. Such was the burgeoning power of the Renault that he was easily past before the hairpin.

And that was pretty much that at the head of the race, as Kovalainen dropped away due to a mismatched set of tyres, leaving the top four to run their own races through the gloom of the Shanghai smog. The Finn's day would only get worse as a puncture dropped him down the order, then a hydraulic problem forced the team to tell him to park up to save his engine for the final race.

The main action at the first corner came behind them, as Jarno Trulli took a look at passing Sebastian Vettel but decided that discretion was the better part of valour and backed off. Only to find the second Toro Rosso, with Sebastien Bourdais at the wheel, diving inside him and slamming into his sidepod, sending both over the kerbs and

Lewis Hamilton was in control and Felipe Massa was only able to keep him from stretching nine points clear by being let into second place.

to the tail of the field. Damaged, Trulli would go little further after a pit stop for repairs failed to do any good.

Hamilton edged ever further clear of Raikkonen, with Massa dropping away as the laps went by. It appeared that Ferrari's problem of getting heat into its tyres was working against them again, until the second half of the stint, when Raikkonen in particular got up to speed. Bear in mind that the Ferraris were on the softer tyres, and this made their problem all the greater.

The first round of pit stops came and went without problem or change of position. It was the same story at the second time of asking, with Hamilton popping out into clear air each time, whereas Raikkonen found himself having to pass slower runners. It made little difference to the outcome though, as the McLaren racer was dominant, not putting a wheel wrong.

In the race's final stint, the expected Ferrari swapping of positions was carried out, rather clumsily, but second place for Massa meant that he would at least have a shot at the title in the season finale on his home circuit. Looking at McLaren's superiority, that would be a mountain to climb, as even a fifth place or higher in Brazil would make Hamilton the youngest ever World Champion.

SHANGHAI ROUND 17

Date: **19 October 2008** Laps: **56** Distance: **189.680 miles/305.250km**
Weather: **Overcast and warm**

RACE RESULT

Position	Driver	Team	Result	Stops	Qualifying Time	Grid
1	**Lewis Hamilton**	McLaren	1h31m57.403s	2	1m36.303s	1
2	**Felipe Massa**	Ferrari	1h32m12.328s	2	1m36.889s	3
3	**Kimi Raikkonen**	Ferrari	1h32m13.848s	2	1m36.645s	2
4	**Fernando Alonso**	Renault	1h32m15.773s	2	1m36.927s	4
5	**Nick Heidfeld**	BMW Sauber	1h32m26.326s	2	1m37.201s	9*
6	**Robert Kubica**	BMW Sauber	1h32m30.622s	2	1m35.814s	11
7	**Timo Glock**	Toyota	1h32m39.125s	1	1m35.937s	12
8	**Nelson Piquet Jr**	Renault	1h32m54.048s	2	1m35.722s	10
9	**Sebastian Vettel**	Toro Rosso	1h33m01.742s	2	1m37.685s	6
10	**David Coulthard**	Red Bull	1h33m12.245s	1	1m36.731s	15
11	**Rubens Barrichello**	Honda	1h33m22.464s	2	1m36.079s	13
12	**Kazuki Nakajima**	Williams	1h33m28.250s	1	1m36.863s	17
13	**Sebastien Bourdais**	Toro Rosso	1h33m28.860s	2	1m38.885s	8
14	**Mark Webber**	Red Bull	1h33m29.825s	2	1m37.083s	16**
15	**Nico Rosberg**	Williams	55 laps	2	1m36.210s	14
16	**Jenson Button**	Honda	55 laps	2	1m37.053s	18
17	**Giancarlo Fisichella**	Force India	55 laps	1	1m37.739s	20
R	**Heikki Kovalainen**	McLaren	49 laps/hydraulics	2	1m36.930s	5
R	**Adrian Sutil**	Force India	13 laps/gearbox	0	1m37.730s	19
R	**Jarno Trulli**	Toyota	2 laps/crash damage	7	1m37.934s	7

FASTEST LAP: HAMILTON, 1M36.325S, 126.587MPH/203.722KPH ON LAP 13
RACE LEADERS: HAMILTON 1-15, 19-56; KOVALAINEN 16-18
* 3-PLACE PENALTY FOR OBSTRUCTING COULTHARD IN Q1. ** 10-PLACE ENGINE-CHANGE PENALTY

TALKING POINT: MOSLEY PITCHES FOR STANDARD ENGINES

FIA President Max Mosley rocked the team principals when he told them that he was putting out to tender a contract to supply all cars with a standard engine. Proposed in his latest round of cost-cutting ideas, it rocked the manufacturer teams who didn't want to lose any advantage they could work for themselves and might remove the reason that manufacturers compete, to beat their rivals. Spec' engines would be cheaper, but F1 fans would also rail at the loss of identity. Among the other proposals was the introduction of standard gearbox internals and standard brake ducts. These were received more favourably by the teams.

Max Mosley made his quest for cost-cutting unacceptable to many by suggesting spec engines.

BRAZILIAN GP

Would it be Lewis Hamilton or Felipe Massa who walked away as champion after a year in which both did their bit to throw it away? The outcome could not have been closer, with Massa driving a perfect race and Hamilton snatching the title.

Overcome by the emotion of his great escape, Lewis Hamilton becomes the centre of world media attention after pipping Massa to the title.

To become World Champion, Massa had to win, Hamilton to finish at least fifth. The other 18 drivers would be bit-parts to these main characters, but it was inevitable that some would be drawn into roles that would put them under the spotlight.

Massa bagged pole position by a clear margin. Hamilton would line up fourth, behind an inspired, but probably fuel-light Jarno Trulli and Kimi Raikkonen who had lapped perhaps a crucial 0.005s faster. This showed the differing ambitions of Massa and Hamilton, but, worryingly, put Hamilton closer to danger, with nemesis Fernando Alonso starting sixth and only team-mate Heikki Kovalainen as a buffer between the two.

As all 20 drivers contemplated their routes to the first corner, the skies opened with a sudden shower. The start was put back 10 minutes and everyone fitted intermediate tyres, except for Kubica who was starting 13th and reckoned he might as well gamble.

Massa got away perfectly, but Hamilton was a little slow off the greasy grid. Fortunately, Kovalainen hung back and ensured that he held fourth into Turn 1. In defending Hamilton from Alonso, he ran wide out of Turn 2 and a fast-starting Vettel was able to get a run on him down to Turn 4. He muscled his Toro Rosso past and Alonso made Hamilton's potential plight worse by getting past as well.

The safety car had already been called for, as Coulthard's final grand prix had been made a short one by a thump from behind by Rosberg that spun him into the path of the other Williams driver, Nakajima.

Force India decided on that opening lap that it would be worth fitting dry tyres to Fisichella's car. Then, once the safety car released the field, the merit of that decision became obvious. It took until lap 9 for any of the frontrunners to follow suit, with Vettel and Alonso coming in. Massa pitted next time around, but Hamilton and McLaren made a mistake by leaving him out for a further lap. Massa had resumed in the lead, but by the time Hamilton came back out, Vettel and Alonso had demoted him and moved by dint of their early stop into second and third. Even Fisichella, up from 19th, was ahead of him.

Hamilton soon demoted Trulli to regain

sixth place, then took a couple of laps to regain fifth from Fisichella, to sighs of relief from McLaren. He was back in the position he needed to be sure of the title.

Up front, Vettel pressed Massa, but when he pitted on lap 27 it became clear that he was not so fast as he was running a three-stop strategy. This was good news both for Massa as it protected his lead and meant that he was battling with Alonso who was 5s further back, but also for Hamilton, as it meant he was effectively fourth.

Then, just when it looked as if Hamilton had done enough, rain hit again with seven laps to go. The tyre changes ran smoothly and Hamilton came out in fifth, but he was struggling for grip, his tyres graining, and Vettel pounced with two laps to go. Disaster for Hamilton, as he was now sixth and would thus finish level on points with Massa but lose the title by dint of having one fewer win.

There was, though, one faint chance. Glock had elected not to change to rain tyres and was nowhere near as fast. The rain intensified on the final lap as Massa roared to victory, sending the crowd into paroxysms of delight, but Glock was now really struggling and Vettel and Hamilton flashed past him with just one corner to go. In an instant, Massa's bubble was popped and a disbelieving Hamilton became the youngest ever World Champion.

INTERLAGOS ROUND 18

Date: **2 November 2008** Laps: **71** Distance: **190.080 miles/305.910km**
Weather: **Wet and warm, then dry then wet**

RACE RESULT

Position	Driver	Team	Result	Stops	Qualifying Time	Grid
1	**Felipe Massa**	Ferrari	1h34m11.435s	3	1m12.368s	1
2	**Fernando Alonso**	Renault	1h34m24.733s	3	1m12.967s	6
3	**Kimi Raikkonen**	Ferrari	1h34m27.670s	3	1m12.825s	3
4	**Sebastian Vettel**	Toro Rosso	1h34m49.446s	4	1m13.082s	7
5	**Lewis Hamilton**	McLaren	1h34m50.342s	3	1m12.830s	4
6	**Timo Glock**	Toyota	1h34m55.803s	2	1m14.230s	10
7	**Heikki Kovalainen**	McLaren	1h35m06.509s	3	1m12.917s	5
8	**Jarno Trulli**	Toyota	1h35m19.898s	2	1m12.737s	2
9	**Mark Webber**	Red Bull	1h35m31.101s	3	1m12.289s	12
10	**Nick Heidfeld**	BMW Sauber	70 laps	3	1m13.297s	8
11	**Robert Kubica**	BMW Sauber	70 laps	3	1m12.300s	13
12	**Nico Rosberg**	Williams	70 laps	3	1m13.002s	18
13	**Jenson Button**	Honda	70 laps	4	1m12.810s	17
14	**Sebastien Bourdais**	Toro Rosso	70 laps	3	1m14.105s	9
15	**Rubens Barrichello**	Honda	70 laps	3	1m13.139s	15
16	**Adrian Sutil**	Force India	69 laps	3	1m13.508s	20
17	**Kazuki Nakajima**	Williams	69 laps	3	1m12.800s	16
18	**Giancarlo Fisichella**	Force India	69 laps	0	1m13.426s	19
19	**Nelson Piquet Jr**	Renault	0 laps/accident	0	1m12.137s	11
20	**David Coulthard**	Red Bull	0 laps/collision	0	1m12.717s	14

FASTEST LAP: MASSA, 1M13.736S, 130.722MPH/210.377KPH ON LAP 36
RACE LEADERS: MASSA 1-9, 12-38, 44-71; TRULLI 10-11; ALONSO 39-40; RAIKKONEN 41-43

TALKING POINT: COULTHARD REACHES THE END OF THE ROAD

David Coulthard hung up his helmet after 247 grands prix, 13 wins and 535 points since he stepped up to race for Williams in 1994 after Ayrton Senna's death.

Four years at Red Bull failed to yield the maiden win that he so wanted to give the team since he joined, but the best he could manage was a couple of podium finishes as the team pulled up short. For this popular Scot's final race, he ran in a car painted in a special livery for Wings for Life, a charity founded by team boss Dietrich Mateschitz to help make spinal paralysis curable. Life will be different as an advisor for Red Bull Racing, a TV pundit and a new father, but his love of racing remains as strong as ever.

It wasn't meant to end like this: DC walks in after being tipped, literally, into retirement.

With the title battle won in the most
dramatic see-saw in racing history,
Lewis Hamilton found himself dazzled
in the middle of a media storm.

FINAL RESULTS 2008

	DRIVER	NAT.		ENGINE	R1	R2	R3	R4
1	LEWIS HAMILTON	GBR	🇬🇧	McLAREN-MERCEDES MP4-23	1P	5	13	3
2	FELIPE MASSA	BRA	🇧🇷	FERRARI F2008	R	RP	1	2
3	KIMI RAIKKONEN	FIN	🇫🇮	FERRARI F2008	8	1	2	1PF
4	ROBERT KUBICA	POL	🇵🇱	BMW SAUBER F1.08	R	2	3P	4
5	FERNANDO ALONSO	SPA	🇪🇸	RENAULT R28	4	8	10	R
6	NICK HEIDFELD	GER	🇩🇪	BMW SAUBER F1.08	2	6F	4	9
7	HEIKKI KOVALAINEN	FIN	🇫🇮	McLAREN-MERCEDES MP4-23	5F	3	5F	R
8	SEBASTIAN VETTEL	GER	🇩🇪	TORO ROSSO-FERRARI STR02B	R	R	R	R
				TORO ROSSO-FERRARI STR03	-	-	-	-
9	JARNO TRULLI	ITA	🇮🇹	TOYOTA TF108	R	4	6	8
10	TIMO GLOCK	GER	🇩🇪	TOYOTA TF108	R	R	9	11
11	MARK WEBBER	AUS	🇦🇺	RED BULL-RENAULT RB4	R	7	7	5
12	NELSON PIQUET JR	BRA	🇧🇷	RENAULT R28	R	11	R	R
13	NICO ROSBERG	GER	🇩🇪	WILLIAMS-TOYOTA FW30	3	14	8	R
14	RUBENS BARRICHELLO	BRA	🇧🇷	HONDA RA108	D	13	11	R
15	KAZUKI NAKAJIMA	JAP	🇯🇵	WILLIAMS-TOYOTA FW30	6	17	14	7
16	DAVID COULTHARD	GBR	🇬🇧	RED BULL-RENAULT RB4	R	9	18	12
17	SEBASTIEN BOURDAIS	FRA	🇫🇷	TORO ROSSO-FERRARI STR02B	7	R	15	R
				TORO ROSSO-FERRARI STR03	-	-	-	-
18	JENSON BUTTON	GBR	🇬🇧	HONDA RA108	R	10	R	6
19	GIANCARLO FISICHELLA	ITA	🇮🇹	FORCE INDIA-FERRARI VJM01	R	12	12	10
20	ADRIAN SUTIL	GER	🇩🇪	FORCE INDIA-FERRARI VJM01	R	R	19	R
21	TAKUMA SATO	JAP	🇯🇵	SUPER AGURI-HONDA SA08	R	16	17	13
22	ANTHONY DAVIDSON	GBR	🇬🇧	SUPER AGURI-HONDA SA08	R	15	16	R

(RACE RESULTS FOR BOTH DRIVERS, ie. FIRST AND SECOND LISTED AS 1/2, WITH THE TEAM'S BETTER RESULT LISTED FIRST)

		SCORING						
			1	FERRARI	8/R	1/R	1/2	1/2
			2	McLAREN-MERCEDES	1/5	3/5	5/13	3/R
1st	10 points		3	BMW SAUBER	2/R	2/6	3/4	4/9
2nd	8 points		4	RENAULT	4/R	8/11	10/R	R/R
3rd	6 points		5	TOYOTA	R/R	4/R	6/9	8/11
4th	5 points		6	TORO ROSSO-FERRARI	7/R	R/R	15/R	R/R
5th	4 points		7	RED BULL-RENAULT	R/R	7/9	7/18	5/12
6th	3 points		8	WILLIAMS-TOYOTA	3/6	14/17	8/14	7/R
7th	2 points		9	HONDA	D/R	10/13	11/R	6/R
8th	1 point		10	FORCE INDIA-FERRARI	R/R	12/R	12/19	10/R
			11	SUPER AGURI-HONDA	R/R	15/16	16/17	13/R

SYMBOLS AND GRAND PRIX KEY

ROUND 1 .... AUSTRALIAN GP   ROUND 7 .... CANADIAN GP   ROUND 13 .... BELGIAN GP
ROUND 2 .... MALAYSIAN GP   ROUND 8 .... FRENCH GP   ROUND 14 .... ITALIAN GP
ROUND 3 .... BAHRAIN GP   ROUND 9 .... BRITISH GP   ROUND 15 .... SINGAPORE GP
ROUND 4 .... SPANISH GP   ROUND 10 .... GERMAN GP   ROUND 16 .... JAPANESE GP
ROUND 5 .... TURKISH GP   ROUND 11 .... HUNGARIAN GP   ROUND 17 .... CHINESE GP
ROUND 6 .... MONACO GP   ROUND 12 .... EUROPEAN GP   ROUND 18 .... BRAZILIAN GP

D DISQUALIFIED   **F** FASTEST LAP   **NC** NOT CLASSIFIED   **NS** NON-STARTER   **P** POLE POSITION   **R** RETIRED   **W** WITHDREW

R5	R6	R7	R8	R9	R10	R11	R12	R13	R14	R15	R16	R17	R18	TOTAL POINTS
2	1	RP	10	1	1P	5P	2	3P	7	3	12P	1PF	5	98
1P	3P	5	1	13	3	17	1PF	1	6	13P	7F	2	1PF	97
3F	9F	RF	2F	4F	6	3F	R	18F	9F	15F	3	3	3	75
4	2	1	5	R	7	8	3	6	3	11	2	6	11	75
6	10	R	8	6	11	4	R	4	4	1	1	4	2	61
5	14	2	13	2	4F	10	9	2	5	6	9	5	10	60
12	8	9	4	5P	5	1	4	10	2	10	R	R	7	53
17	-	-	-	-	-	-	-	-	-	-	-	-	-	
-	5	8	12	R	8	R	6	5	1P	5	6	9	4	35
10	13	6	3	7	9	7	5	16	13	R	5	R	8	31
13	12	4	11	12	R	2	7	9	11	4	R	7	6	25
7	4	12	6	10	R	9	12	8	8	R	8	14	9	21
15	R	R	7	R	2	6	11	R	10	R	4	8	R	19
8	R	10	16	9	10	14	8	12	14	2	11	15	12	17
14	6	7	14	3	R	16	16	R	17	R	13	11	15	11
R	7	R	15	8	14	13	15	14	12	8	15	12	17	9
9	R	3	9	R	13	11	17	11	16	7	R	10	R	8
R														
-	R	13	17	11	12	18	10	7	18	12	10	13	14	4
11	11	11	R	R	17	12	13	15	15	9	14	16	13	3
R	R	R	18	R	16	15	14	17	R	14	R	17	18	0
16	R	R	19	R	15	R	R	13	19	R	R	R	16	0
-	-	-	-	-	-	-	-	-	-	-	-	-	-	0
-	-	-	-	-	-	-	-	-	-	-	-	-	-	0

R5	R6	R7	R8	R9	R10	R11	R12	R13	R14	R15	R16	R17	R18	TOTAL POINTS
1/3	3/9	5/R	1/2	4/13	3/6	3/17	1/R	1/18	6/9	13/15	3/7	2/3	1/3	172
2/12	1/8	9/R	4/10	1/5	1/5	1/5	2/4	3/10	2/7	3/10	12/R	1/R	5/7	151
4/5	2/14	1/2	5/13	2/R	4/7	8/10	3/9	2/6	3/5	6/11	2/91	5/6	10/11	135
6/15	10/R	R/R	7/8	6/R	2/11	4/6	11/R	4/R	4/10	1/R	1/4	4/8	2/R	80
10/13	12/13	4/6	3/11	7/12	9/R	2/7	5/7	9/16	11/13	4/R	5/R	7/R	6/8	56
17/R	5/R	8/13	12/17	11/R	8/12	18/R	6/10	5/7	1/18	5/12	6/10	9/13	4/14	39
7/9	4/R	3/12	6/9	10/R	13/R	9/11	12/17	8/11	8/16	7/R	8/R	10/14	9/R	29
8/R	7/R	10/R	15/16	8/9	10/14	13/14	8/15	12/14	12/14	2/8	11/15	12/15	12/17	26
11/14	6/11	7/11	14/R	3/R	17/R	12/16	13/16	15/R	15/17	9/R	13/14	11/16	13/15	14
16/R	R/R	R/R	18/19	R/R	15/16	15/R	14/R	13/17	19/R	14/R	R/R	17/R	16/18	0
-	-	-	-	-	-	-	-	-	-	-	-	-	-	0

FORMULA 1 RECORDS

MOST GRANDS PRIX STARTS

DRIVERS

270	Rubens Barrichello	(BRA)
256	Riccardo Patrese	(ITA)
250	Michael Schumacher	(GER)
247	David Coulthard	(GBR)
214	Giancarlo Fisichella	(ITA)
210	Gerhard Berger	(AUT)
208	Andrea de Cesaris	(ITA)
204	Nelson Piquet	(BRA)
202	Jarno Trulli	(ITA)
201	Jean Alesi	FRA)
199	Alain Prost	(FRA)
194	Michele Alboreto	(ITA)
187	Nigel Mansell	(GBR)
180	Ralf Schumacher	(GER)
176	Graham Hill	(GBR)
175	Jacques Laffite	(FRA)
171	Niki Lauda	(AUT)

165	Jacques Villeneuve	(CDN)
163	Thierry Boutsen	(BEL)
162	Mika Hakkinen	(FIN)
	Johnny Herbert	(GBR)
161	Ayrton Senna	(BRA)
159	Heinz-Harald Frentzen	(GER)
158	Martin Brundle	(GBR)
	Olivier Panis	(FRA)
154	Jenson Button	(GBR)
152	Nick Heidfeld	(GER)
	John Watson	(GBR)
149	Rene Arnoux	(FRA)
147	Eddie Irvine	(GBR)
	Derek Warwick	(GBR)
146	Carlos Reutemann	(ARG)
144	Emerson Fittipaldi	(BRA)
140	Kimi Raikkonen	(FIN)

135	Jean-Pierre Jarier	(FRA)
132	Eddie Cheever	(USA)
	Clay Regazzoni	(SUI)
128	Mario Andretti	(USA)
126	Jack Brabham	(AUS)
123	Fernando Alonso	(SPA)
	Ronnie Peterson	(SWE)
122	Mark Webber	(AUS)
119	Pierluigi Martini	(ITA)
116	Damon Hill	(GBR)
	Jacky Ickx	(BEL)
	Alan Jones	(AUS)
114	Keke Rosberg	(FIN)
	Patrick Tambay	(FRA)
112	Denny Hulme	(NZL)
	Jody Scheckter	(RSA)

CONSTRUCTORS

776	Ferrari
649	McLaren
568	Williams
490	Lotus
418	Tyrrell
409	Prost
394	Brabham
394	Toro Rosso (nee Minardi)
383	Arrows
317	Benetton
303	Force India (nee Jordan then Midland then Spyker)
270	BMW Sauber
246	Renault
230	March
206	Red Bull (nee Stewart then Jaguar Racing)
197	BRM
171	Honda Racing (nee BAR)
132	Osella

Giancarlo Fisichella began his career with Minardi in the 1996 Australian GP and is still going.

Jackie Stewart gets his Tyrrell airborne in the 1973 German GP at the Nurburgring en route to his 27th and final win.

MOST GRANDS PRIX WINS

DRIVERS

91	Michael Schumacher	(GER)	14	Jack Brabham	(AUS)	9	Rubens Barrichello	(BRA)
51	Alain Prost	(FRA)		Emerson Fittipaldi	(BRA)		Lewis Hamilton	(GBR)
41	Ayrton Senna	(BRA)		Graham Hill	(GBR)	8	Denny Hulme	(NZL)
31	Nigel Mansell	(GBR)	13	Alberto Ascari	(ITA)		Jacky Ickx	(BEL)
27	Jackie Stewart	(GBR)		David Coulthard	(GBR)	7	Rene Arnoux	(FRA)
25	Jim Clark	(GBR)	12	Mario Andretti	(USA)		Juan Pablo Montoya	(COL)
	Niki Lauda	(AUT)		Alan Jones	(AUS)	6	Tony Brooks	(GBR)
24	Juan Manuel Fangio	(ARG)		Carlos Reutemann	(ARG)		Jacques Laffite	(FRA)
23	Nelson Piquet	(BRA)	11	Felipe Massa	(BRA)		Riccardo Patrese	(FRA)
22	Damon Hill	(GBR)		Jacques Villeneuve	(CDN)		Jochen Rindt	(AUT)
21	Fernando Alonso	(SPA)	10	Gerhard Berger	(AUT)		Ralf Schumacher	(GER)
20	Mika Hakkinen	(FIN)		James Hunt	(GBR)		John Surtees	(GBR)
17	Kimi Raikkonen	(FIN)		Ronnie Peterson	(SWE)		Gilles Villeneuve	(CDN)
16	Stirling Moss	(GBR)		Jody Scheckter	(RSA)			

CONSTRUCTORS

209	Ferrari	9	Ligier		Eagle
162	McLaren		Maserati		Hesketh
113	Williams		Matra		Honda Racing (nee BAR)
79	Lotus		Mercedes		Penske
35	Brabham		Vanwall		Porsche
	Renault	4	Force India (nee Jordan then		Scuderia Toro Rosso
27	Benetton		Midland then Spyker)		Shadow
23	Tyrrell	3	March		Red Bull (nee Stewart then
17	BRM		Wolf		Jaguar Racing)
16	Cooper	2	Honda		
10	Alfa Romeo	1	BMW Sauber		

Nigel Mansell had already been crowned world champion when he raced to the ninth win of his campaign at Estoril in 1992.

MOST GRANDS PRIX WINS IN ONE SEASON

DRIVERS

13	Michael Schumacher	(GER)	2004
11	Michael Schumacher	(GER)	2002
9	Nigel Mansell	(GBR)	1992
	Michael Schumacher	(GER)	1995
	Michael Schumacher	(GER)	2000
	Michael Schumacher	(GER)	2001
8	Mika Hakkinen	(FIN)	1998
	Damon Hill	(GBR)	1996
	Michael Schumacher	(GER)	1994
	Ayrton Senna	(BRA)	1988
7	Fernando Alonso	(SPA)	2005

	Fernando Alonso	(SPA)	2006
	Jim Clark	(GBR)	1963
	Alain Prost	(FRA)	1984
	Alain Prost	(FRA)	1988
	Alain Prost	(FRA)	1993
	Kimi Raikkonen	(FIN)	2005
	Ayrton Senna	(BRA)	1991
	Jacques Villeneuve	(CDN)	1997
6	Mario Andretti	(USA)	1978
	Alberto Ascari	(ITA)	1952
	Jim Clark	(GBR)	1965

	Juan Manuel Fangio	(ARG)	1954
	Damon Hill	(GBR)	1994
	James Hunt	(GBR)	1976
	Nigel Mansell	(GBR)	1987
	Felipe Massa	(BRA)	2008
	Kimi Raikkonen	(FIN)	2007
	Michael Schumacher	(GER)	1998
	Michael Schumacher	(GER)	2003
	Michael Schumacher	(GER)	2006
	Ayrton Senna	(BRA)	1989
	Ayrton Senna	(BRA)	1990

CONSTRUCTORS

15	Ferrari	2004
	Ferrari	2002
	McLaren	1988
12	McLaren	1984
	Williams	1996
11	Benetton	1995
10	Ferrari	2000
	McLaren	2005
	McLaren	1989
	Williams	1992
	Williams	1993
9	Ferrari	2001

	Ferrari	2006
	Ferrari	2007
	McLaren	1998
	Williams	1986
	Williams	1987
8	Benetton	1994
	Ferrari	2008
	Ferrari	2003
	Lotus	1978
	McLaren	1991
	McLaren	2007
	Renault	2005

	Renault	2006
	Williams	1997
7	Ferrari	1952
	Ferrari	1953
	Ferrari	2008
	Lotus	1963
	Lotus	1973
	McLaren	1999
	McLaren	2000
	Tyrrell	1971
	Williams	1991
	Williams	1994

MOST POLE POSITIONS

DRIVERS

68	Michael Schumacher	(GER)
65	Ayrton Senna	(BRA)
33	Jim Clark	(GBR)
	Alain Prost	(FRA)
32	Nigel Mansell	(GBR)
29	Juan Manuel Fangio	(ARG)
26	Mika Hakkinen	(FIN)
24	Niki Lauda	(AUT)
	Nelson Piquet	(BRA)
20	Damon Hill	(GBR)
18	Mario Andretti	(USA)
	Rene Arnoux	(FRA)
17	Jackie Stewart	(GBR)
16	Fernando Alonso	(SPA)
	Stirling Moss	(GBR)
	Kimi Raikkonen	(FIN)
15	Felipe Massa	(BRA)
14	Alberto Ascari	(ITA)
	James Hunt	(GBR)
	Ronnie Peterson	(SWE)
13	Rubens Barrichello	(BRA)
	Jack Brabham	(AUS)
	Lewis Hamilton	(GBR)
	Graham Hill	(GBR)
	Jacky Ickx	(BEL)
	Juan Pablo Montoya	(COL)
	Jacques Villeneuve	(CDN)
12	Gerhard Berger	(AUT)
	David Coulthard	(GBR)
10	Jochen Rindt	(AUT)
8	Riccardo Patrese	(ITA)
	John Surtees	(GBR)

CONSTRUCTORS

203	Ferrari
141	McLaren
125	Williams
107	Lotus
50	Renault
39	Brabham
16	Benetton
14	Tyrrell
12	Alfa Romeo
11	BRM
	Cooper
10	Maserati
9	Prost
8	Mercedes
7	Vanwall
5	March
4	Matra
3	Honda Racing (nee BAR)
	Shadow
2	Force India (nee Jordan then Midland then Spyker)
	Lancia
	Toyota
1	BMW Sauber
	Red Bull (nee Stewart then Jaguar Racing)
	Scuderia Toro Rosso

Lotus team chief Peter Warr greets Ayrton Senna after his first victory in Portugal in 1985.

MOST FASTEST LAPS

DRIVERS

75	Michael Schumacher	(GER)
41	Alain Prost	(FRA)
35	Kimi Raikkonen	(FIN)
30	Nigel Mansell	(GBR)
28	Jim Clark	(GBR)
25	Mika Hakkinen	(FIN)
24	Niki Lauda	(AUT)
23	Juan Manuel Fangio	(ARG)
	Nelson Piquet	(BRA)
21	Gerhard Berger	(AUT)
19	Damon Hill	(GBR)
	Stirling Moss	(GBR)
	Ayrton Senna	(BRA)
18	David Coulthard	(GBR)
15	Rubens Barrichello	(BRA)
	Clay Regazzoni	(SUI)
	Jackie Stewart	(GBR)
14	Jacky Ickx	(BEL)
13	Alberto Ascari	(ITA)
	Alan Jones	(AUS)
	Riccardo Patrese	(ITA)
12	Rene Arnoux	(FRA)
	Jack Brabham	(AUS)
	Juan Pablo Montoya	(COL)
11	Fernando Alonso	(SPA)
	Felipe Massa	(BRA)
	John Surtees	(GBR)

CONSTRUCTORS

217	Ferrari
137	McLaren
129	Williams
71	Lotus
40	Brabham
35	Benetton
27	Renault
20	Tyrrell
15	BRM
	Maserati
14	Alfa Romeo
13	Cooper
12	Matra
11	Prost
9	Mercedes
7	March
6	Vanwall

Lotus racer Jim Clark sets the second of his 28 fastest laps at Monaco in 1962.

Alain Prost celebrates winning the 1985 British GP. He would lift three titles and have the most points until Michael Schumacher came along.

MOST POINTS (THIS FIGURE IS GROSS TALLY, I.E. INCLUDING SCORES THAT WERE LATER DROPPED)

DRIVERS

1369	Michael Schumacher	(GER)
798.5	Alain Prost	(FRA)
614	Ayrton Senna	(BRA)
541	Fernando Alonso	(SPA)
535	David Coulthard	(GBR)
531	Kimi Raikkonen	(FIN)
530	Rubens Barrichello	(BRA)
485.5	Nelson Piquet	(BRA)
482	Nigel Mansell	(GBR)
420.5	Niki Lauda	(AUT)
420	Mika Hakkinen	(FIN)
385	Gerhard Berger	(AUT)
360	Damon Hill	(GBR)
	Jackie Stewart	(GBR)
329	Ralf Schumacher	(GER)
310	Carlos Reutemann	(ARG)
307	Juan Pablo Montoya	(COL)
298	Felipe Massa	(BRA)
289	Graham Hill	(GBR)
281	Emerson Fittipaldi	(BRA)
	Riccardo Patrese	(ITA)
277.5	Juan Manuel Fangio	(ARG)
274	Jim Clark	(GBR)
267	Giancarlo Fisichella	(ITA)
261	Jack Brabham	(AUS)
255	Jody Scheckter	(RSA)
248	Denny Hulme	(NZL)

CONSTRUCTORS

4021.5	Ferrari	
3301.5	McLaren	
2571.5	Williams	
1352	Lotus	
1056	Renault	
877.5	Benetton	
854	Brabham	
617	Tyrrell	
468	BMW Sauber	
439	BRM	
424	Prost	
333	Cooper	
326	Honda Racing (nee BAR)	
288	Force India (nee Jordan then	
	Midland then Spyker)	
219	Toyota	
171.5	March	
191	Red Bull (nee Stewart then	
	Jaguar Racing)	
167	Arrows	
155	Matra	

MOST DRIVERS' TITLES

7	Michael Schumacher	(GER)	Jim Clark	(GBR)	Denis Hulme	(NZL)
5	Juan Manuel Fangio	(ARG)	Emerson Fittipaldi	(BRA)	James Hunt	(GBR)
4	Alain Prost	(FRA)	Mika Hakkinen	(FIN)	Alan Jones	(AUS)
3	Jack Brabham	(AUS)	Graham Hill	(GBR)	Nigel Mansell	(GBR)
	Niki Lauda	(AUT)	**1** Mario Andretti	(USA)	Kimi Raikkonen	(FIN)
	Nelson Piquet	(BRA)	Giuseppe Farina	(ITA)	Jochen Rindt	(AUT)
	Ayrton Senna	(BRA)	Lewis Hamilton	(GBR)	Keke Rosberg	(FIN)
	Jackie Stewart	(GBR)	Mike Hawthorn	(GBR)	Jody Scheckter	(RSA)
2	Fernando Alonso	(SPA)	Damon Hill	(GBR)	John Surtees	(GBR)
	Alberto Ascari	(ITA)	Phil Hill	(USA)	Jacques Villeneuve	(CDN)

Michael Schumacher celebrates the first of his seven world titles at Adelaide in 1994 after his controversial clincher for Benetton.

Ferrari is way out front in terms of constructors' titles. Here, Lorenzo Bandini laps Giancarlo Baghetti's Centro Sud BRM in the 1964 Dutch GP.

MOST CONSTRUCTORS' TITLES

16	Ferrari		Cooper		Tyrrell
9	Williams		Renault		Vanwall
8	McLaren	**1**	Benetton		
7	Lotus		BRM		
2	Brabham		Matra		

NB TO AVOID CONFUSION, THE RENAULT STATS LISTED ARE BASED ON THE TEAM THAT EVOLVED FROM BENETTON IN 2002 AND INCLUDE THOSE STATS THAT HAVE HAPPENED SINCE PLUS THOSE FROM RENAULT'S FIRST SPELL IN F1 BETWEEN 1977 AND 1985. THE FIGURES FOR BENETTON AND TOLEMAN FROM WHICH IT METAMORPHOSED IN 1986 ARE LISTED AS BENETTON. CONVERSELY, THE STATS FOR RED BULL INCLUDE THOSE OF THE STEWART AND JAGUAR RACING TEAMS FROM WHICH IT EVOLVED. LIKEWISE, FORCE INDIA'S STATS INCLUDE THOSE OF JORDAN, MIDLAND SPYKER AND SCUDERIA TORO ROSSO THOSE OF MINARDI.

2009 FILL-IN CHART

DRIVER	TEAM	Round 1 29 March AUSTRALIAN GP	Round 2 5 April MALAYSIAN GP	Round 3 19 April CHINESE GP	Round 4 26 April BAHRAIN GP	Round 5 10 May SPANISH GP	Round 6 24 May MONACO GP	Round 7 7 June TURKISH GP
1 LEWIS HAMILTON	McLaren	4						
2 HEIKKI KOVALAINEN	McLaren							
3 FELIPE MASSA	Ferrari							
4 KIMI RAIKKONEN	Ferrari							
5 ROBERT KUBICA	BMW Sauber							
6 NICK HEIDFELD	BMW Sauber							
7 FERNANDO ALONSO	Renault							
8 NELSON PIQUET JR	Renault							
9 JARNO TRULLI	Toyota	3						
10 TIMO GLOCK	Toyota							
11 TAKUMA SATO*	Toro Rosso							
12 SEBASTIEN BUEMI	Toro Rosso							
14 MARK WEBBER	Red Bull							
15 SEBASTIAN VETTEL	Red Bull							
16 NICO ROSBERG	Williams							
17 KAZUKI NAKAJIMA	Williams							
18 JENSON BUTTON	Team X	1						
19 ~~BRUNO SENNA~~* BARRICHELLO	Team X	2						
20 GIANCARLO FISICHELLA*	Force India							
21 ADRIAN SUTIL*	Force India							

SCORING SYSTEM: 10, 8, 6, 5, 4, 3, 2, 1 POINTS
FOR THE FIRST EIGHT FINISHERS IN EACH GRAND PRIX
*TO BE CONFIRMED AT THE TIME OF GOING PRESS

Round 8 21 June BRITISH GP	**Round 9** 12 July GERMAN GP	**Round 10** 26 July HUNGARIAN GP	**Round 11** 23 August EUROPEAN GP	**Round 12** 30 August BELGIAN GP	**Round 13** 13 Sept ITALIAN GP	**Round 14** 27 Sept SINGAPORE GP	**Round 15** 4 October JAPANESE GP	**Round 16** 18 October BRAZILIAN GP	**Round 17** 1 November ABU DHABI GP		**POINTS TOTAL**	

PICTURE CREDITS

Eventual champ Lewis Hamilton, Robert Kubica and Felipe Massa were the main men in 2008.

The publishers would like to thank the following sources for their kind permission to reproduce the pictures in this book.

Getty Images: /Bay Ismoyo/AFP: 54-55

LAT Photographic: 118, 119, 120, 121, 122, 123, 124, 125; /Lorenzo Bellanca: 79, 87; /Charles Coates: 18, 19, 21, 23, 27, 36, 44, 47, 48, 83, 91, 95, 98, 99, 112; /Glenn Dunbar: 10, 11, 17, 20, 24, 29, 34, 40, 46, 70, 88, 92, 108, 110; /Steve Etherington: 31, 84, 85, 90, 94, 96, 100, 104, 107; /FOM: 101; /Andrew Ferraro: 8-9, 12, 14, 15, 16, 22, 25, 26, 28, 30, 35, 38, 39, 41, 42, 43, 49, 52-53t, 59, 78, 80, 81, 86, 89, 93, 97, 102, 105, 106, 109, 113; /Jean Michel Le Meur/DPPI: 103; /Alastair Staley: 32, 33, 45; /Steven Tee: 2-3, 4, 6-7, 13, 37, 52-53b, 53t, 53b, 76-77, 82, 111, 128; /www.abudhabigp.com: 75

PA Photos: /Sutton Motorsport: 114-115

Illustrations courtesy of **Graphic News**.

Every effort has been made to acknowledge correctly and contact the source and/or copyright holder of each picture and Carlton Books Limited apologises for any unintentional errors or omissions, which will be corrected in future editions of this book.